THE SKY'S THE LIMIT

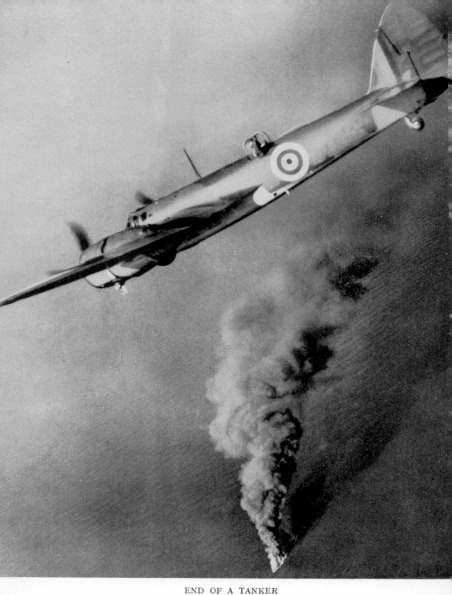

END OF A TANKER

An R.A.F. bomber watches the end of an enemy Tanker, as, ablaze from stem to stern, she sinks in the Channel off the French Coast.

(*Official Photograph*)

THE SKY'S THE LIMIT

A STUDY OF BRITISH AIR POWER

BY

J. M. SPAIGHT,

C.B., C.B.E.

LONDON
HODDER AND STOUGHTON

First Printed . . . . *August, 1940*

*Made and Printed in Great Britain for Hodder & Stoughton Limited, London
by Wyman & Sons Limited, London, Reading and Fakenham*

CONTENTS

CHAPTER   PAGE

1. BRITAIN RULED THE AIR - - - - 11
The First Mastery—The Roll Call of
Honour—Striking Power.

2. THE YEARS BETWEEN - - - - - 22
The Foundations Stood—The Power
Returns—The "Shadow Factories"—
Factories at War.

3. THE EMPIRE TAKES WINGS - - - - 39
The Great Plan—Canada and Australia—
Air Forces of the Dominions—U.S.A.

4. THE SPLENDID MACHINES - - - - 55
"The Best in the World"—The Battle of
Designs—The Bombers—The Fighters—
Armour and Guns—Fighter *versus* Bomber.

5. THE MEN OF THE AIR - - - - 74
Airmanship wins—R.A.F.—R.A.F.V.R.—
A.A.F.—Airmen in the making.

6. BOMBERS AT WORK - - - - - 89
The Acid Test—Dive-bombing and
"precision"—The Whitley rejuvenated
—Security Patrol—The bombers get busy
—The Bridge at Maastricht.

CONTENTS

CHAPTER   PAGE

7.   FIGHTERS IN ACTION - - - - -   105
   Check to the Bomber—The Fighter Command—Defending Britain's Coasts—St. George's Dragons—An Epic of Norway—Enter the Defiant.

8.   THE COASTAL COMMAND - - - -   124
   Endless Vigil—Convoys and Flying Boats—The Fleet Air Arm—Air and Sea.

9.   AIR FORCE OVERSEAS - - - - -   134
   South and East—B.E.F.—Air and The Army—Lessons from Spain and France—Victory at Dunkirk.

10.   PAST AND FUTURE - - - - -   146
    The Bowmen began it—The power that Grows—The command of the air.

INDEX - - - - - - -   157

LIST OF ILLUSTRATIONS

	FACING PAGE
End of a Tanker - - - *Frontispiece*	
Sir Cyril Newall - - - - -	12
Sir Edgar Ludlow-Hewitt - - - - -	13
Dawn Patrol - - - - - -	16
Anti-Aircraft Practice - - - -	17
London's Anti-Aircraft Defences - - -	32
Anti-Aircraft Gun - - - - -	33
Hurricanes in the Making - - - - -	36
An Aircraft Factory - - - - -	37
Fairey Battles under Construction - - -	44
H.M. the King with a " Readiness " Squadron -	45
New Zealand Airmen - - - - -	45
Handley Page Hampden - - - - -	48
Bombing Up - - - - - -	49
Australian Airmen - - - - -	52
Bristol Beaufort Bomber - - - -	53
Spitfires - - - - - - -	60
Vickers Wellesley Bomber - - - - -	61
A Vickers Wellington Bomber - - - -	64
Bristol Blenheim in Flight - - - -	65
The Flying Classroom - - - - -	68
Aircraftmen in Training - - - - -	69
Apprentices under Instruction - - - -	69
Operations - - - - - -	76
The Link Trainer - - - - -	76
Miles Master - - - - - -	77
The Harvard - - - - - -	77

9

LIST OF ILLUSTRATIONS

	FACING PAGE
R.A.F. Fighter Aircraft on the Western Front -	80
Airspeed Oxford - - - - -	80
The Photograph Speaks - - - -	81
Whitley Bomber - - - - -	96
The Sting in the Tail - - - -	97
Sharp Shooters of the Air - - - -	100
Ground Defences - - - - -	100
Target Practice - - - - -	101
The New Fleet " Spotter " - - -	101
Defiants on the Wing - - - -	108
The Defiant's Turret - - - -	109
Waiting for the Word - - - -	109
Wreckage of a Messerschmitt - - -	116
Blackburn Skuas - - - - -	117
The Fleet Air Arm's New Fighter - -	124
Convoy and Patrol - - - -	125
Short Sunderland - - - - -	125
Saro-Lerwick - - - - -	128
Short Sunderland - - - - -	128
Torpedo Bombers - - - - -	129
Torpedo - - - - - -	132
End of a Dornier - - - - -	133
Avro Ansons - - - - -	140
On the Western Front - - - -	141
H.M.S. *Ark Royal* - - - -	144
With the Fleet Air Arm - - - -	144
Food from the Air - - - - -	145
A Fleeing Dornier - - - - -	145
Rheine, Westphalia - - - -	150
A German Aerodrome - - - -	151
Hudsons over Heligoland - - -	154
End of a Heinkel - - - - -	154
The End of a German Bomber - - -	155

CHAPTER I

BRITAIN RULED THE AIR

THE FIRST MASTERY

WE are witnessing in these days a great drama which is in the nature of a revival, a re-setting on a grander scale of an earlier spectacle. The last generation saw the creation of British air power. We are privileged to-day to assist in its re-creation. For the second time in our history we are seeking in the air above us the source of that national strength which, from the time of the seventh Henry onwards, we have found in the sea around us ; and to-day we have an Empire to aid us in the quest.

In 1918 Britain was the strongest Power in the air. That position was not won easily or quickly. We had a rough road to travel. In August, 1914, our air strength was less than that of France or of Germany. The four squadrons of the Royal Flying Corps which took the field in August, 1914, were a patchwork body. Two of them were equipped with British machines—B.E.2's. The others had to depend in whole or part upon French machines—Blériots and Henri Farmans. Moreover, not a single one of them all had a British engine. Every machine in our squadrons had a French engine installed in it, mainly the Gnome rotary of

80 horse power. The British aircraft industry was almost non-existent. It was wholly unable to meet even the modest needs of the tiny expeditionary force of the air which left these shores in the first month of the last war.

Steadily we built up a mighty structure of air strength. We owed much to France in the early days. Indeed, for a substantial part of the war we relied upon France for aero-engines and to a less extent for airframes also. Many thousands of French engines had to be obtained for installation in our machines during 1915 and 1916. Aircraft, too, were supplied in considerable quantities from the same source. The Nieuport fighters helped us out of a tight corner more than once. Our total purchases of foreign aircraft, however, amounted to only a little more than 3,000 machines in the four years of war, as compared with 17,000 engines purchased abroad. It was only in the last year or so of the war that we became wholly independent of France for aeronautical equipment. Seeing how we started in 1914, one can only feel amazement that we should have ended the war with the magnificently equipped air force which we then possessed, predominant in quality as well as in quantity. It was a wonderful effort, when all is said and done.

When the war began we had on charge in the Royal Flying Corps and Royal Naval Air Service 218 land aeroplanes, 52 seaplanes and 7 airships, but less than 100 of the aeroplanes were in a condition to take the air. There were 276 officers and 1,797 other ranks in the two Services. Our production of aircraft during the first twelve months of the war averaged 50 a month, that of engines 14 a month. At the end of

SIR CYRIL NEWALL
Air Chief Marshal Sir Cyril Newall, Chief of the Air Staff.

SIR EDGAR LUDLOW-HEWITT
Air Chief Marshal Sir Edgar Ludlow-Hewitt,
Inspector General of the Royal Air Force.

the war we compared as follows with France and Germany, the two powers nearest to us in air strength :

I

Total number of aeroplanes on charge in November, 1918 :

Great Britain	..	22,171
France ..	..	15,342
Germany	..	14,731

II

Number of pilots and observers in November, 1918 (approximate figures) :

Great Britain	..	20,100
France ..	..	16,000
Germany	..	11,000

III

Production in 1918 :

		Aircraft		Engines
Great Britain	..	26,685	..	29,561
France ..	..	23,669	..	44,563
Germany	..	14,386	..	16,412

IV

Total production, 1914–1918 :

		Aircraft		Engines
Great Britain	..	55,093	..	41,034
France ..	..	67,982	..	85,317
Germany	..	47,637	..	40,449

Tables III and IV above are particularly significant. They show clearly that our graph of production was rising and Germany's falling. Our output of aircraft in 1918 was nearly 50 per cent. of our total output during the four years of war. Germany's output in 1918 was only 30 per cent. of her total production. We must have out-distanced her completely in the air if the war had continued into 1919. We had won the battle of the workshops and that meant, in turn, winning the battle in the air. Behind our immense production and France's there stood, moreover, the rising output of the United States. In 1918 about 12,000 aircraft and 31,000 engines were manufactured in that country : an extraordinary achievement, for America, it must be remembered, started from scratch in April, 1917. She had practically no aircraft industry at the time when she became involved in the war. To-day the position is very different. America has an immense aircraft industry now, and her productive capacity is as fully at our call as it was in 1918. The first call upon it is, of course, for her own re-armament, but then that call was even more insistent in 1918. It is possible that the assistance which we can obtain from the United States, in the shape of aeronautical equipment and the materials for such equipment, will prove to be as vital a factor in this war as her actual intervention was in the last.

An American expert has calculated that the United States will be supplying Britain and France (and France's contracts have now been taken over by Britain) with over 5,000 machines in 1940, that that number could be increased to 8,000, approximately, if extra plant capacity were taken into use, and that by the spring of 1941 the United States will be producing aircraft of fighting types for foreign delivery at the rate of nearly 1,000 a month.[1] Even at present, it was stated by an informed correspondent at Washington, the American aircraft industry is capable of producing 1,800 aeroplanes a month.[2] A far greater production than this was foreshadowed by Lord Beaverbrook, Minister for Aircraft Production, in a broadcast on 24th July, 1940, when he stated that a new American programme was being approved which would yield 3,000 machines a month to Britain. Mr. Morgenthau, the Secretary of the Treasury, stated that the United States would give every facility for the supply of 72,000 aircraft to Britain in the two years, 1941 and 1942. Yet the American industry will be merely, for us, an extra source of supply ; its output will be completely overshadowed by our own.

No country in the world was in possession of such a formidable air force as was Britain in the closing months of the last war. In quality of equipment we held an undoubted lead. There were fine machines, too, in the French and German air forces, for all that they, like ours of that time, were made of silver spruce and very different from the all-metal stressed-skin machines of to-day. They did their job ; they had engine failures, to-day hardly ever experienced ; they had no speed to speak of ; but they fought and bombed, and that was what mattered. The Spad, the Nieuport, the Fokker D VII, the Albatros, the Halberstadt were

[1] Major G. F. Eliot, in *Life*, quoted in *The Times*, 6th January, 1940.

[2] *The Times*, 10th January, 1940. President Roosevelt has expressed the view that the production of the United States should be increased to 50,000 aircraft *per annum*.

fighters of which France and Germany had good reason to be proud; yet we had machines of better performance still in the Snipe and the S.E.5A. In the bomber class, too, we had no reason to fear any comparison. The D.H.9A among light bombers, the Handley Page among heavy, were the best of their time. There was no finer co-operation machine than the Bristol Fighter (it was not a fighter, for all its name, in the strict sense). For ten years the " Brisfit " remained a standard machine in the Royal Air Force; over 3,000 of the type were produced. Our aero-engines, too, were unsurpassed. They were puny things compared with the 1,000 horse-power engines of to-day, but, again, they were good for their time. The Napier Lion of 450 horse power, which did good service in the Royal Air Force for many years, was only in production at the time of the armistice, but the Rolls-Royce engines of 250 and 275 horse power were in use, and the same constructors' bigger engine of 375 horse power was installed in the four-engined super-Handley Pages which were to have bombed Berlin if the war had continued. These were water-cooled engines; in the air-cooled class our Bentley Rotary engines of 230 horse power were equally pre-eminent.

From 1917 onwards, said Lord Weir, who had been Secretary of State for Air in 1918, " the performance of our aeroplanes was very undoubtedly in advance of that of the Germans, who were cramped by their non-elastic engine policy."[1] " In 1918 we were incomparably the best equipped of all nations in the

[1] Paper read at Newcastle on 10th July, 1919, quoted in *Flight*, 31st July, 1919.

DAWN PATROL.

(Official Photograph)

ANTI-AIRCRAFT PRACTICE

Anti-Aircraft units with their guns in training, showing the crew loading up one of the guns ready for firing at a target towed by aircraft, in the West of England.

(*Photo : Keystone*)

air," said General Seely (now Lord Mottistone), also a former Air Minister, on 8th June, 1920.

THE ROLL CALL OF HONOUR

If the machines were good, the men in them were better. Was there ever such a company of heroes as that Air Force of ours ? Their names come crowding on the memory, and each is a bugle-call : Mannock, Ball, McCudden, Bishop, Barker, Lanoe, Hawker, Collishaw, Little, Dallas and a host of others. They were gluttons for fight. They went out looking for trouble. The British airmen, said Von Richthofen, never refused combat—they were brave to the point of "stupidity." Was there ever such a mad, glorious, immortal fight as that which W. G. Barker fought over the Fôret de Mormal on 27th October, 1918 ? He fought, single-handed, about forty or fifty Fokker fighters, shot down four of them, possibly six, and, terribly wounded, succeeded in shaking them all off and landing his machine in the Allies' lines. He survived that fight, which recalls Grenville and the *Revenge*, only to be killed, alas ! in a flying accident at Ottawa on 12th March, 1930 ; he was a Canadian. So, too, was Bishop, who headed the list of British "Aces" and still survives. There were men from every Dominion in that wonderful Air Force of 1918, but the "hard centre" of it was British.

Its motto was attack—attack all the time. One has heard it again in these days, on the lips of one of the present Air Officers Commanding-in-Chief : "Never decline combat." It is not surprising to hear such an echo from the past. The men now in command—the Air Marshals—Newall, Dowding, Ludlow-Hewitt, Longmore, Burnett, Barratt, Bowhill, Mitchell—were bred in that school of 1914–18. They learnt their fighting then. They served under Trenchard, and Trenchard it was who, above all, made that Force the cutting edge of battle which it was. He commanded the Royal Flying Corps in France from August, 1915, until January, 1918, when he became Chief of the Air Staff in the newly formed Air Ministry—a post which he held at that time for only a few months, though later in the year he was appointed to it again and held it for ten years. In June, 1918, he was given the command of the Independent Air Force.

STRIKING POWER

It was a maxim of Lord Trenchard's, and the writer heard it from his own lips, that ten bombers can be made to do the work of thirty, or of a hundred. All that is needed is to send them in again and again. Have you had heavy losses in your first raid ? Then launch another, and your losses will be less ; a third, and they will probably be *nil*. Why ? Because the fighters will be back upon the ground. And it is not the destruction of life or property which the bombers cause that matters ; it is the destruction of *morale*, the disturbance of life, the dislocation of routine. The moral effect is far more important than the material. Keep on raiding : that is the right strategy in the air, according to the Trenchard school.

One thinks of Foch : *Mon centre cède, ma droite*

recule. Tout va bien. J'attaque. That might have
been the maxim of the Independent Force. It had
grave losses, but it kept on. It was never a large
Force, and it was constantly being diverted to other
uses than that for which it was intended.

Sir Frederick Sykes, who was Chief of the Air Staff
in 1918, has written that " only a comparatively small
percentage of the efforts of the Independent Air Force
were directed against the industrial targets for which
the force had been created."[1]

Another and latter authority has thus described the
situation to which Sir Frederick Sykes refers :

" The most significant piece of specialization, after
being mooted for more than a year, was realized too
late to be given a thorough test. This was the plan
for the creation of the Independent Force of the
R.A.F. . . . There were great plans in the Independent Force when the war ended. . . . They were
never accomplished, and it has to be admitted that
the complete policy of the Independent Force was
not fully tested."[2]

Because British air power did not accomplish more
in 1918 than it did, there is a tendency to assume that
it cannot accomplish much now. Yet it had its re-
sounding successes then. In the west it had no such
opportunities as in the eastern theatres of war. It
smashed up the Second Bulgarian Army in the Kresna
Pass, the retreating Austrians on the Conegliano-
Pordenone road, the Seventh Turkish Army on the

[1] Sir Frederick Sykes, *Aviation in Peace and War*, 1922, p. 92.
[2] E. Colston Shepherd, *The Air Force of To-day*, 1939, pp. 64–65.

Neblus-Jordan road, in September and October, 1918. In the west the belligerents were too evenly matched in the air to allow the possibilities of *predominant* air power to be fully exploited. The Independent Force was never strong enough. It consisted of only nine bombing squadrons and one fighter squadron. The last, a Sopwith Camel squadron, was added to the Force only in September, 1918.

There was no great disparity in 1918 between the first-line strengths of France, Britain and Germany,[1] and the chief call upon the air effectives of all the belligerents came from the armies, for reconnaissance and other tactical duties close to the front. If the war had gone on for another year or more, certainly if it had grown into a second " Seven Years' War," the enormous strength in the air which Britain, France and the United States would have amassed before the end would have allowed the Allies' air arms to be used independently or " strategically," and must have had a decisive influence upon the course of the war. The advantage which the defence enjoys in the air (as, indeed, on land, too) would have been swamped by the swelling, overflowing torrent of attack which could have been brought against it. The lesson of the Polish campaign of September, 1939, would have been learnt about twenty years earlier. The world would have been given a demonstration of what air power—air power that is really such—can achieve. As it was, the world, having been given no such demonstration, was left with the false impression that air power was,

---

[1] They were : France, 3,600 ; Britain, 3,300 ; Germany, 3,000, all approximately. Britain, however, had the greatest number of aircraft in reserve.

after all, ineffective, or, at all events, that it could not accomplish what its champions claimed.

It is not easy to resurrect dead history to recall these facts. They have a bearing upon the situation to-day. In 1918 Britain was the strongest Power in the air : the strongest, but only just the strongest. What happened then is no proof that it will happen again if, now, Britain becomes by far, and beyond question, the strongest Power in the air : Britain, that is to say, as an Empire, Britain as the leader and centre of the team of nations which intends to storm the enemy's goal. Will the defence prevail against that attack ? It will be a colossal onslaught. The effect which we made in 1918 was but a feeble one in comparison with that which we, which the British nations as a whole, are making now. And we have the great plants of California and other States in America to supplement our own and the Dominions' enormous production. The end of it all can hardly be doubtful.

CHAPTER 2

THE YEARS BETWEEN

THE FOUNDATIONS STOOD

So stood British air power in 1918. How did it stand
on the brink of another war in 1939 ? Not, certainly,
in the same relative position to the fated opponent,
yet upon foundations whose solidity gave promise that
an even greater edifice of air power might yet be reared
upon them. Those foundations were laid in the years
1936 to 1939, and to understand the position as it was
at the beginning of September in the latter year it is
necessary to go back a little and to explain briefly what
happened in the few preceding years.

We laid the foundations of the second great structure
of air power in those years, but already, before that
time, we had in fact cleared the way for the expansion ;
or, perhaps one should say, we had kept ready and
tended the ground which had been prepared in 1917–18,
when air power was organised first on an adequate
basis in this country. We had already in existence
the nucleus or central cell round which the greater
growth could develop easily and almost naturally.
Everything had to be duplicated, quadruplicated when
the need for expansion arose, but at least there was
already in being the unit which had to be multiplied.

That was an enormous advantage at the start. We had something upon which to build, and it was sound, good stuff, with nothing shoddy or makeshift in its composition. We had preserved the organisation of 1918, and—which was as important—we had not relaxed the high standard of quality that was then set. There was no improvisation, there was simply a development of an existing organisation and an existing force. We had taken care, too, to preserve the designing ability and constructional experience of the aircraft industry. The Air Ministry was often criticised in the years before 1935 for spreading its orders among so many as fourteen or fifteen constructors of aircraft and four engine firms. If it had not done so, some of them would have gone out of existence and their very capable staffs would have turned to other work. The wisdom of the Department in " nursing " the constructional firms was seen when re-armament became necessary.

It was fortunate, too, that research and development were never given up in those years of slack business. We sought always for improved performance and better and better results. The fact that the Air Ministry was concerned with civil as well as military aviation was a decided advantage in this respect. It had the result that the two branches of aeronautics could be so co-ordinated that any improvement or advance in one could be utilised for the advantage of the other also. A practical example will illustrate the inter-connection.

Anyone who happened to be in the north of the Isle of Wight, as the writer was, in the autumn of 1929 would have seen and heard a very wonderful

thing. It was a silvery meteor—a horizontal meteor—
which flashed over Spithead and was gone, with a
sibilant roar, almost before the watcher realised its
passing. It was the British seaplane, the entrant for
the Schneider Trophy, flying at the amazing speed
(for that day) of 358 miles an hour. But it was something else, too. If the watcher had been gifted with
prophetic vision he would have seen and heard a
different scene and sound : a Spitfire hurtling over the
Firth of Forth with its eight guns crackling and spitting
fire into the tail of a German Heinkel, sending it to
its doom, shattered and helpless. Ten years later that
second scene was staged and much water flowed under
the bridges meanwhile, yet the two events were closely
inter-related.

The Spitfire—its airframe a Supermarine, its engine
a Rolls-Royce product—is in the true line of descent
from that low-wing monoplane which shrieked its way
across Spithead in 1929 ; and the Hurricane is a very
near relative. Two years later another competition
was held ; Lady Houston's generosity and patriotism
enabled us to enter again in that year of financial stress ;
and the Schneider Trophy was finally won by Great
Britain, but won by a machine—the Supermarine-
Rolls-Royce S.6B., which had been designed for the
earlier contest. It was the machine used in 1929—the
S.6—which set the new standard in the air. It was
proof of the practicability of the levitation of an enor-
mously powerful engine on a small wing and fuselage,
so streamlined that speeds formerly considered incredible
could be attained.

The policy which we adopted in the years before
the expansion was a necessary and an immediately

fruitful one ; necessary, because in no other way could it be secured that this country would be able to cope with the greatly enhanced rapidity of production and volume of output which would be required in a future war ; fruitful, because we did in fact lead the world in performance and, among other things, in the development of the new all-metal technique in those years. It is true that the Air Force itself was allowed to shrink to a size which, in the retrospect, can now be seen to have been unjustifiably low ; but the risk which we ran in thus almost disarming ourselves in the air was, perhaps, one worth incurring in the cause of world peace. This is not the place, in any event, to discuss the question whether we were wise or not in letting the level of our air strength fall below that of some other great Powers. It is worth recording, however, what the position was before our re-armament began.

In 1923 the Government had decided that a Home Defence Air Force of fifty-two squadrons was necessary for our security and that such a force should be completed by 1928. Actually, by 1933, only forty-two squadrons had been formed ; in the years 1932 and 1933 not a single unit was added to the establishment. In February, 1934, we had 850 first-line aircraft in all (at home and overseas) as compared with France's 1,650. We were, at all events, better off than ten years earlier. On 14th March, 1924, Sir Samuel Hoare, then Secretary of State for Air, had informed an apparently unimpressed House of Commons that " to-day we have 371 first-line machines as compared with 3,300 in November, 1918." How were the mighty fallen !

THE POWER RETURNS

It was in 1934 that we began to re-arm, reluctantly and in a very small way at first. The Air Estimates in that year provided for the formation of four new squadrons, to be followed by eleven more in 1935–36. Events in Europe led to successive enlargements of this initial programme. *Scheme F* of 1936, which would have given us a total of about 2,700 first-line aircraft, at home, afloat and abroad, was succeeded by *Scheme L*, which raised the total to 3,360 ; then, in November, 1938, came *Scheme M*, which increased the number to about 3,550. This (*Scheme M*) was the programme on which we were working when the present war began, but obviously it has had to be put in the melting pot again since then. What total strength we are aiming at now can only be a matter for conjecture, and of undesirable conjecture. It is clearly a much greater strength than that which *Scheme M* would have given us ; and *Scheme M*, it will be noted, would have given us more first-line aircraft, all told, than we had in 1918. Ministers have stated that a new and greatly increased plan of production was put into operation upon the outbreak of war. Probably our war programme is limited only by the capacity of our production ; and as to this Sir Kingsley Wood stated on 7th March, 1940, that " every month new plant is coming into operation." It is a fairly safe conclusion that the first-line strength which will result from it will leave our establishment of November, 1918, far behind.

The magnitude of our effort in 1939 may be judged from the fact that the Air Estimates for that year amounted to the colossal total of £207,000,000. They had been just over £17,000,000 in 1932. Of the £207,000,000 to be spent in 1939-40, no less than, approximately, £115,000,000 was for technical equipment (Vote 3) ; and in March, 1939, we were spending £250,000 a day in aircraft alone.[1] The expenditure on aircraft in 1940 will probably be an almost astronomical figure ; the Estimates give no guidance as to its magnitude, since only a token sum of £100 is taken in each Vote, the war expenditure being financed from a Vote of Credit. What appropriation there will be from this Vote for air services can only be a matter of guess-work. All that Sir Kingsley Wood said upon this particular point when introducing the Air Estimates in the House of Commons on 7th March, 1940, was that they were " of unprecedented character and involved by far the greatest effort and expenditure ever made by this country in any year in relation to our air defences."

The fact that we, on our side, began the war in 1939 with a total air strength not far short of that which we possessed in 1918 was of less moment than another and less commonly appreciated fact, namely that our aircraft industry had practically been put on a war footing long before zero hour. We had by that date already organised a system of production comparable to that which it took three years to develop in 1914-18. In those years we had to create and then expand an aircraft industry capable of meeting the ever-increasing needs of our air squadrons in the field, and to do so under the stress of war conditions and subject to all the handicaps which the submarine and, to a less extent, the air bombing operations of the enemy imposed upon

[1] Statement of Sir Kingsley Wood in House of Commons on 9th March, 1939.

us. In 1936–38 we were able to build up our manufacturing strength without let or hindrance ; in fact,
to do before war began what we had had to do after it
began on the previous occasion. That was a very great
advantage at the start.

It was only one of various ways in which we were
wiser in 1939 than we had been in 1914. In 1914, for
instance, we had depended on Germany for some
vitally important raw materials such as ferro-tungsten
as well as for such supplies as optical glass and magnetos ; the only good magnetos were then made by
Bosch or by Eisemann. Again, we had no machine-
tool industry worth speaking of in 1914. In 1939 the
British tool-making industry was efficient and well-
organised, and from 1936 onwards we had taken the
precaution to obtain very large supplies of machine-
tools from the United States, the most important
manufacturing centre of this essential basis of large-
scale production of armaments.

THE " SHADOW FACTORIES "

It was in 1936, too, that the " shadow factories "
were organised, for the manufacture of airframes and
aero-engines. It had already been decided that certain
large engineering firms, which were not engaged
ordinarily in armament work, would be called upon in
an emergency to undertake the production of munitions
and thus to supplement the normal source of supply.
The firms in question were allocated in advance to the
three services, naval, military and air ; those ear-marked
for the production of aircraft and engines were motor

manufacturing firms. When, in March, 1936, it was decided greatly to enlarge the existing programme of expansion of the Royal Air Force, the supplies required under the new programme were found to be considerably in excess of the capacity of the score of firms already engaged in manufacturing aircraft and aero-engines. It would have been possible in these circumstances to have met the needs of the new situation by granting financial assistance to the firms already making aircraft and engines, to enable them to increase their capacity. The alternative course, which the Government adopted, was to bring new firms into the ring of specialised construction and thus to widen the source of supply. This course meant anticipating in peace the change-over to a system which it had been intended to bring into operation only upon the outbreak of war.

There were two advantages to be gained by the adoption of the plan in question. First, it would enable the reserves of aircraft and engines required under the scheme of expansion to be provided more quickly than if they had been included in contracts placed with the regular suppliers ; secondly, it would give the engineering firms allocated to the Air Ministry experience which would be invaluable when the system of war production had to be put into operation. New factories were accordingly erected at the cost of the Air Ministry, the necessary machine-tools and other plant were installed, and arrangements were made for the engineering firms concerned to manage the new factories as agents for the Air Ministry. The firms were paid for the aircraft and engines produced at rates agreed between the Government and themselves. The prices were so fixed as to ensure that an excess profit was in no case made, however large the output. In most instances the new factories were close to those of the managing firm, whose work of supervision was thus facilitated, while the problem of labour supply was also largely solved by the location of the new plants in areas in which there was already an engineering tradition. The shadow factories were, in fact, brought into production in an extraordinarily short space of time. In October, 1937, it was possible to show them, already turning out airframes and engines, to General Milch, the German Secretary of State for Air, and his mission, who happened then to be visiting this country.

The firms undertaking the construction of airframes, were the Austin Motor Co., Ltd., and Rootes Securities Ltd. (the firm controlling the Humber-Hillman-Commer combine), and the types entrusted to them were the Fairey Battle and the Bristol Blenheim, respectively. The same two firms participated in the scheme of engine construction also, the other firms here concerned being the Daimler Co., the Rover Co., and the Standard Motor Co. Each of these firms undertook to build certain parts of the engine selected for manufacture—the Bristol Mercury—and the assembly and testing of the complete engine were entrusted to the Austin Motor Co. and the Bristol Aeroplane Co.; the latter firm agreed to come into the team after Wolseley Motors Ltd., who were at first to have shared the work of assembling with the Austin Co., decided to withdraw. A special factory was built at the Government's expense for the Bristol Co. for this purpose.

The shadow factories were not confined to airframes and engines; there were others for the manufacture of variable pitch propellers, carburetters and bombs.

There were, in addition, a number of factories which were not " shadow," that is to say, factories erected and financed under the arrangements referred to above. Among these other factories the most important were those erected by Lord Nuffield for the construction of Spitfire fighters, supplementing the " parent " Vickers-Supermarine works, and by Rolls-Royce Ltd. for the construction of Merlin engines as overflow-factories from their original works. New factories or extensions to existing factories were also put in hand by a large number of aircraft firms—Airspeed, Armstrong-Whitworth, Blackburn Aircraft, Fairey, Gloster, Hawker, Handley Page, Phillips and Powis, A. V. Roe, Short Bros., Harland (Belfast), Vickers-Armstrong, and Westland Aircraft.

Many of these new and enlarged factories were turning out their products in the spring of 1939. " There is a substantial output," it was stated in the Memorandum accompanying the Air Estimates for 1939–40, " from the Government factories established in accordance with the policy announced in 1936 ; this is increasing rapidly." To meet the new needs arising under the expanded programmes of May and November, 1938, the Memorandum added, productive capacity was again being increased. " This capacity is being provided partly by the extended use of sub-contracting ; partly by additions to existing factories ; partly by the erection of new factories to be managed by large engineering firms not previously concerned with the manufacture of aircraft ; and partly by capacity to be developed in the overseas Dominions." Among the large engineering firms here referred to as being brought into the aircraft industry may be mentioned the Metropolitan

Vickers Electrical Co., the English Electric Co., Associated Electrical Industries, and Vickers-Armstrong.

The measures referred to in the Memorandum, quoted above, for increasing output were reinforced by an administrative change made within the Air Ministry itself. At the beginning of 1939 a Directorate-General of Production was created, and under the Director-General's control Directorates were formed to deal with the production of aeroplanes, engines, aircraft equipment, instruments, armaments and materials, and with sub-contracting, statistics and planning, war planning and Air Ministry factories. The Directorate of Research was transformed into a Directorate-General of Research and Development, controlling Directorates of technical development, scientific research, aircraft development, communication development, and repairs and maintenance.

The Directorate-General of Production was replaced by a new and still higher authority shortly after Sir Samuel Hoare had succeeded Sir Kingsley Wood as Air Minister in the spring of 1940. The Air Ministry announced on 22nd April that Sir Charles Craven, of Vickers Ltd., would join the Air Council as Civil Member for Development and Production. He would also be chairman of the Air Supply Board, of which the deputy Chairman would be Lord Riverdale, while the two Air Marshals responsible, on the Air Council, for Development and Production and for Supply and Organisation, respectively, would be members of the Board, with some other representatives of industry and the Ministry. In commenting upon this change, *The Times* said (23rd April) :—

LONDON'S
ANTI-AIRCRAFT
DEFENCES

The searchlight unit
in action. In the
foreground is sil-
houetted the sound
locator which enables
the beam of light to
be directed to the
target.

(Photo: Sport &
General Press Agency
Ltd.)

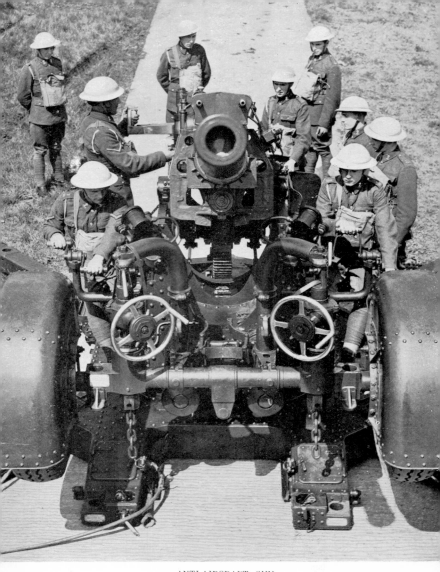

ANTI-AIRCRAFT GUN

In this remarkable photograph, taken from above, the camera
is looking right down the muzzle of a deadly 3.7 gun.

(*Photo: Sport & General Press Agency Ltd.*)

Though no figures can be published, every day the production of British aircraft is steadily going up. Still bigger production plans are envisaged, and the target to-day is higher than that aimed at, say, three months ago. Indeed, when the figures are ultimately made known, it is believed that they will be " almost astronomical." Personnel is keeping pace with the enormous increase in the number of aircraft, and the labour supply has so far proved satisfactory, though very soon further big demands on the labour market will have to be met. More factories and more aerodromes are rapidly being built, for the Government are determined to get and keep the mastery of the air.

A still more important change followed upon Mr. Churchill's succession to the Premiership. On 15th May, 1940, it was announced that Lord Beaverbrook had been appointed Minister for Aircraft Production. This was a new post, corresponding, within the limitations implied in its title, to the Minister for Munitions, who was responsible during the last war for the production of (*inter alia*) aircraft and aero engines. The creation of the new Ministerial post was a recognition of the great importance attached to the securing of the maximum output of aeronautical equipment. Lord Beaverbrook was able to report on 7th July, 1940, that our production of aircraft in June constituted a record and was twice as great as in June, 1939.

Already, under Sir Kingsley Wood's administration, an immense programme of construction had been put in hand and had made great progress. A panel of industrial advisers had been appointed to ensure close

co-operation between the Department and the manu-
facturers. Everything possible was done to secure that
the flow of orders should be as smooth and unbroken
as was practicable, with due regard to the exigencies
of the service and the need for improved types, that
the firms' manufacturing capacity should be utilised to
the full, and that there should be no gap between
successive contracts. Planning ahead and the placing
of large orders were important features of the policy
adopted for the purpose of ensuring the greatest possible
output.

The " group system " of production was one of the
means adopted for increasing the output of aircraft.
As explained by Sir Kingsley Wood in the House of
Commons on 9th March, 1939, it involved the brigading
of three or four firms in a group or team, with which
an order was placed for the manufacture of a particular
type of aircraft, the work of construction being split
up between the firms in the group. The object was
to reduce the number of designs in service and to
facilitate the economical and rapid production of aircraft
in quantities. It made large-scale planning and ordering
possible, and was calculated to reduce the dislocation
which might otherwise arise in war if for any reason
one of the manufacturing team were unable to continue
production. The system was applicable alike to the
firms ordinarily engaged in aircraft construction, to
the Government factories, and to the new factories
which were being erected by Metropolitan Vickers and
others.

In addition to extended resort to sub-contracting,
the adoption of the system of " split assembly " was
another valuable aid to rapid production. It was

designed to overcome the difficulties presented by the manufacture of the stressed-skin all-metal machines which are now generally in use. Under this system the metal skin is attached to the framework at an early stage in the process of manufacture, and it is possible, therefore, to complete the separate construction of wings and fuselages before they are brought together for assembly. Combined with the intensive use of jigs and tools, the system has the effect of reducing congestion of workpeople in the main factory at each stage of construction and leads to a substantial saving of the man-hours involved in the manufacture of an aircraft.[1]

FACTORIES AT WAR

Mr. Chamberlain stated at the Dorchester Hotel in January, 1940, that more people were now employed in the industry than at the peak of our output in the last war, yet even this tremendous force will be trebled or quadrupled before long. That was, indeed, implied in Sir Kingsley Wood's speech, on the Air Estimates, in the House of Commons on 7th March, 1940. He repeated Mr. Chamberlain's statement that we had already passed the peak figure of labour employed on aircraft production in the last war—we did so, he said, within a few weeks of the outbreak of war—and added that " there was an enormous programme required and an even greater effort ahead."

Sufficiency of machine-tools, of light metal alloys, of skilled labour : this is the basis of the structure of air

[1] Paper by Sir Charles Bruce Gardner in *Air Annual of the British Empire*, 1939, p. 10.

power. War is waged to-day in the factory and the workshop before it is waged in the field. The stage of intensive arming precedes the stage of encounter. Industrial mobilisation must come before military mobilisation. If it does not, the military effort may be held up at a vital stage. Zero hour in war to-day is that at which the war industries of the belligerents come into full blast, and the problem is how to reduce the gap between that time and the (earlier) time at which military operations may have begun.

To meet this danger it had been suggested, in the light of the experience gained in the last war, that we in this country should accumulate a reserve of aircraft amounting to as much as 500 per cent. of our first-line strength.[1] That figure was based on the assumption that wastage would be about 80 per cent. a month and that a period of six months at least, possibly twelve, would elapse before the switch-over from peace-time to full war-time production was completed. Actually, of course, because of the course which this war has taken, the wastage has been nothing like 80 per cent. In any case, the measures which we adopted in 1936 to 1939 had the effect of shortening very considerably the dangerous *interim* period to which Mr. H. A. Jones refers. By inaugurating the shadow factory scheme and otherwise putting our industries on a *semi*-war basis before the war, we took steps to reduce the size of the gap which would otherwise have constituted a grave defect in our defences if no action had been taken until 3rd September.

Meanwhile, concurrently with the drive to equip the new squadrons of the Royal Air Force and the Auxiliary

[1] H. A. Jones, *The War in the Air*, Vol. VI, Chapter II.

HURRICANES IN THE MAKING

One of the many West of England factories where "Hurricane" Fighters are produced.

(Photo: Sport & General Press Agency Ltd., London)

AN AIRCRAFT FACTORY

Blenheim bombers under construction. This huge factory represents only a very small fraction of Britain's enormous output of aircraft.

(*Photo: Central Press Photos Ltd.*)

Air Force and to re-equip the existing squadrons, the building of new stations and the enlargement of existing stations to house them was going on at a rapid pace. A great programme of building construction was taken in hand in 1936. A large number of fine aerodromes, each capable of accommodating two or three units, were constructed, mainly in the eastern half of Great Britain. New Armament Training Camps, for bombing and gunnery practice at coastal ranges, also sprang up. Additional Flying Training Schools were formed, while arrangements were made at the same time for providing new or increased facilities for initial training at civil flying schools. The progress made on this side was no less remarkable than that witnessed in the other spheres of the expansion.

The re-armament which we put in hand in 1936 failed in its larger purpose but succeeded in a secondary (but very important) one. It did not avail to prevent war—which was what we most desired—but it did place this country in a position in which attack upon it from the air became a very much more dangerous adventure than it would have been if we had done nothing in those years to strengthen our defences. We had almost invited attack as we stood in the preceding years. By September, 1939, both our active close defence and our counter-offensive strength had become so formidable that the bombing of this country could be seen to be a very dubious proposition for any enemy, however strong in the air. It was that, probably, which saved London from being sunk without trace. We had created at least a balance of air power, and for that we must be supremely thankful. On the other hand, we had not built up our air strength to the point at which it was wise for us to set a hot pace in the air. We, no less than the enemy, had to think twice about initiating a *régime* of long-range raiding and the bombing of the enemy's hinterland. Hence the strange lull in the air during the first eight months of this war of surprises.

Our own policy of restraint was defended by Lord Chatfield, the Minister for the Co-ordination of Defence, in his speech at Cardiff on 17th February, 1940. " I am convinced," he said, " that our air policy has been correct and wise. We have gained valuable time to build up our own strength for attack and for the defence of these islands. *We shall bring our great and ever-growing strength into play at the right instant*." The tremendous resources of the British Commonwealth of Nations are now devoted to the task of creating " air forces of overwhelming strength," and it is reasonable to assume that they will be used to overwhelm. The bombers which we are building can hardly be intended to be kept as museum pieces.

CHAPTER 3

THE EMPIRE TAKES WINGS

The Great Plan

THINK of a number; double it: one knows the old game. Think of the Royal Air Force as it will emerge from the effort which Great Britain is making now. Think of the machines being turned out of the great workshops in their thousands, of the airmen being trained in thousands, too, of the vast accumulation of air strength in which our scheme of expansion and production will result. Think of the sum of it all as a number, and then *double* that number. What then? That is not an idle question, nor is the supposition behind it an idle one. The question answers itself readily for those who have hearkened to Gilbert Chesterton's " voice valedictory—Who is for Victory? Who is for Liberty? " The supposition is a reality that is taking shape—the reality of the Empire air effort.

The Empire air scheme in its magnitude was conceived only in 1939, but the foundations of it had been laid in 1938. In August of that year Sir Hardman Lever, Air Chief-Marshal Sir Edward Ellington, and other British representatives visited Canada, the purpose of the visit being to arrange for the manufacture in that country of long-range bombing aircraft for the Royal

Air Force and also to investigate the possibility of the construction of other types of aircraft there. The result was the placing of an order for the production of Hampden twin-engined bombers in Canada ; the head of the firm which produces this type in the United Kingdom, Mr. Handley Page, was a member of the Lever mission and his advice was available in regard to the manner in which the manufacture of the machine could most effectively be approached. Subsequently orders were placed for the construction of some other types, including Hurricane[1] fighters and Lysander co-operation machines, and also another bomber the particulars of which have not yet been made public ; its existence has been hinted at only. The Bolingbroke, a version of the Blenheim, is also being built for the Royal Canadian Air Force. The arrangements made by the Lever mission with the Canadian authorities provided for an increase in the capacity of a number of aircraft factories already in existence in Canada, namely, those of the Canadian Car and Foundry Co., the National Steel Car Corporation, Canadian Vickers, the Ottawa Car Manufacturing Co., Fleet Aircraft, and the Fairchild Aircraft Company. These companies, it was agreed, should manufacture the components of the Hampden, which would be assembled at two new factories to be built at Montreal and Toronto. To manage the assembling factories and to organise production as a whole a new central company was set up under the title of " Canadian Associated Aircraft Ltd." ; its directing body included representatives of the firms referred to above.

[1] The first Hurricane built under the scheme was delivered in Great Britain on 29th February, 1940.

When the Empire air scheme was inaugurated in October, 1939, the group system of production in Canada was organised on a still greater scale. Sir Kingsley Wood stated at Bristol on 10th February, 1940 : " I am glad to be able to say that not only are we employing on a considerable scale Canadian aircraft firms in the production of different types of aircraft for the Royal Air Force, but the group organisation which we have established as a result of the mission to Canada in 1938 has now been greatly extended and entrusted with further orders to the value of, roughly, £6,000,000 for covering the production of aircraft of the latest type." In addition to the Hampdens, Lysanders and Hurricanes already referred to, Fleet Trainers, Tiger Moths and Harvard Trainers are being manufactured in Canada for the purposes of the scheme.

CANADA AND AUSTRALIA

The establishment of an important aircraft industry in Canada had been mooted by experts from time to time, for instance, by Captain Norman Macmillan and M. C. Rougeron. The former had criticised the policy of locating our shadow factories in areas in the United Kingdom which might prove vulnerable to attack and had suggested that aircraft manufacture should be transferred to Canada.[1] M. Rougeron had drawn attention to one of the lessons of the civil war in Spain and its bearing upon the problem of aeronautical supply with which Britain and France would be

[1] N. Macmillan, *The Chosen Instrument*, 1938, p. 164.

faced in any future war.[1] The Spanish Republicans, he pointed out, had begun by controlling all the armament factories and metallurgical plants in the country, yet the advantage which they thus possessed was entirely lost before the war had lasted for any length of time. The reason was that the Nationalist aviation, which had command of the air, set before itself as a primary aim the destruction of the enemy's war industry. " It must be recognised that the repeated bombardments to which the munitions factories of the Spanish Government were subjected were the chief cause of their feeble production."

If there should be large-scale bombing the location of a substantial proportion of our aircraft industry in regions far removed from danger will be a vitally important advantage to us, and might even be decisive, since it is an advantage completely denied to our enemies. " Opinions," said Sir Kingsley Wood in a speech to the Empire Press Union on 26th June, 1939, " might very well differ as to the possibilities of devastating cities by air attack, but there could only be one answer to the possibility of devastating an entire Empire."

The possibility of the bombers made in Canada being delivered under their own power to this country was in the minds of our Ministers when the proposal to build aircraft for the Royal Air Force in Canada was first considered. " In war," said Lord Swinton in the House of Lords on 12th May, 1938, " Canada might and would become a very valuable source of supply for this country. And with the great range

[1] C. Rougeron, *Les Enseignements Aériens de la Guerre d'Espagne*, 1939, pp. 142–3.

which aircraft are now attaining it would be more than possible to build in Canada aircraft which would not need to be taken to pieces and put in a ship, but which it would be possible to fly across the Atlantic. I believe that to be a very real possibility." The Hampdens which were to be built in Canada, said Sir Thomas Inskip on 17th November, 1938, could be flown across the Atlantic " in never-ending waves."

In January, 1939, Sir Hardman Lever, Air Marshal Sir Arthur Longmore and Sir Donald Banks, the Secretary of the Air Ministry, visited Australia. Their mission was undertaken, it was stated in the official announcement, " for the purpose of examining in consultation with representatives of the Commonwealth Government the possibility of the creation of further capacity for the production of aircraft in the Commonwealth and to prepare a scheme for the consideration of both Governments." The object in view, said Mr. Lyons, the Premier of Australia, was to develop Australian industry to a stage at which it could produce all Australian defence and aviation requirements and meet also those of New Zealand and a proportion of those at Singapore in an emergency. Great Britain, it was well stated in an Australian newspaper,[1] was thinking of Australia as an aeroplane arsenal for the South Pacific and of strengthening the link in the chain of aerial defence of New Zealand, Singapore and even India. The immediate result of the visit was the placing of an order for the manufacture of Beaufort machines—a development of the Blenheim—in the Commonwealth. One hundred of these machines

[1] *Sunday Morning Herald*, quoted in *The Times*, 31st December, 1938.

were to be completed in the first year and production of 800 a year was contemplated eventually. The engines for installation in it (Bristol Taurus) were to be obtained from Great Britain, but the manufacture of these also in Australia was envisaged as a later development.

There was already in existence in Australia a young but flourishing aircraft plant, that of the Commonwealth Aircraft Corporation at Fishermen's Bend, near Melbourne. It was producing the Wirraway two-seater general purpose machine, an adaption of the American N.A.33. This plant it was decided to expand so that it could assemble a greatly increased number of aircraft, the parts of which would be built by sub-contractors. In addition to the Wirraway, the Beaufort reconnaissance-bomber was also selected for manufacture. This machine lent itself to a system of dispersed manufacture, being specially designed for easy and rapid production under a system which permitted the components to be built up in successive assemblies, so that diffusion of construction was practicable. The parts were to be built by sub-contractors, and sub-assembly of the sections of the airframe was to be carried out at the railway workshops in New South Wales, Victoria, Queensland, and South Australia. Final assembly was to take place at Melbourne and Sydney. Tiger Moth training machines and the Gypsy engines for them are also manufactured in Australia (as well as in Canada and New Zealand) by the De Havilland Aircraft Company.

The Lever mission went on from Australia to New Zealand in the early Spring of 1939. Here, too, their visit paved the way for the bigger scheme which was

FAIREY BATTLES
UNDER
CONSTRUCTION

One of the many
"Shadow" factories.

(Photo:
" The Aeroplane")

H.M. THE KING WITH A " READINESS " SQUADRON
There is always a " readiness " squadron at a Fighter Command aerodrome ready to take off at a moment's notice.
(*Official Photograph*)

NEW ZEALAND AIRMEN
Members of the unit march past the High Commissioner for New Zealand.
(*Official Photograph*)

to take shape in the following October. The mission recommended that the New Zealand Government should place orders for the manufacture in that country of training aircraft by the De Havilland Company, who would establish a factory there. A further recommendation was that training facilities in New Zealand should be expanded so that an increased output of fully trained flying *personnel* should be available for the air forces of both New Zealand and Great Britain in peace and in war. For some time a limited number of Dominion pilots had been trained in their own countries for the Royal Air Force, in which they came to serve for a few years before returning to their home forces. It is interesting to note that one of the pilots of the Royal Air Force decorated for gallantry in the present war was a New Zealander who was so trained. He was Pilot Officer G. W. F. Carey, who was awarded the Distinguished Flying Cross for skill and gallantry in an encounter with enemy aircraft over the North Sea in January, 1940 ; he shot down one in flames and damaged another. He had been given a year's training in New Zealand before he came to Great Britain to join the Royal Air Force about twelve months before the date of the award.

AIR FORCES OF THE DOMINIONS

It will be seen that even before the present war began the Empire had set itself to the task of organising its air power for the struggle whose coming was already foreseen. The Dominions had themselves air forces which, though small, were very highly trained and well equipped, and units of the Australian and Canadian air forces have already come to our aid in the present war.[1] They were mostly in process of being re-organised when the war began. The Royal Australian Air Force, which had consisted of five regular and three cadre squadrons, was to have been expanded into nineteen operational squadrons by 1940 ; it will be a far larger force now that war has come. The Royal Canadian Air Force was composed of eight permanent and eleven non-permanent squadrons and was also being increased ; again, the outbreak of war will have the effect of making the expansion an immensely greater one than had been contemplated. In South Africa, whose Air Force consisted of four operational and five training squadrons in March, 1939, plans had been drawn up for the formation of twelve bomber and fighter squadrons, to be manned by the Active Citizens' Defence Force trained under the "Thousand pilots' scheme" formulated by Mr. Pirow. The New Zealand Air Force which had been reorganised as a result of the visit of Marshal of the Royal Air Force Sir John Salmond in 1928, was also being expanded both on the regular and the territorial side. Sir John Salmond, it may be added, also visited Australia, and his suggestions for an expansion of the Royal Australian Air Force had already been adopted before 1939.

The various increases in establishments which were thus in train, important as they were, were completely overshadowed by the great scheme of expansion agreed upon and announced after the present war began.

---

[1] The first squadron of the Royal Australian Air Force landed in this country on 26th December, 1939 ; the first squadron of the Royal Canadian Air Force on 25th February, 1940.

Everything that had gone before seemed, indeed, to be but a feeble effort in comparison with that to which the British Empire braced itself when the actual trial of strength began. It is in truth a wonderful conception, the Empire air scheme. In its possibilities it is the biggest thing yet attempted in this war. " I do not believe," said Mr. Eden, when Secretary of State for the Dominions, " that its significance has yet been realised." It was " a magnificent conception," " a scheme of which the importance cannot possibly be over-emphasised," said Sir Archibald Sinclair, Secretary of State for Air, in a broadcast to the Empire on 17th July, 1940.

It is primarily a scheme for the provision of *personnel* for the British and Dominion Air Forces but embraces production of *matériel* as well. It is not always borne in mind that an even larger production of *personnel* is involved in any scheme of air expansion. Air warfare consumes far more men than machines. The " crew " of a fighter is normally one man only, the pilot ; that of a bomber may vary from two to six men. Each loss of a bomber on a raid means, therefore, that a heavier call has be to made upon the reserve of *personnel* than upon the reserve of *matériel* to make good the loss. As Mr. Menzies stated in his broadcast to the people of Australia on 11th October, the problem of decisive air action is not only a mechanical one ; a country might be producing more aircraft than it could competently fly. " The Empire Governments," he said, " were determined that this should not happen to us, but that the vast air armada we are preparing should be manned by courageous airmen whose morale would be sustained till victory was achieved."

"The undertaking," said Sir Kingsley Wood in the House of Commons on 10th October, when he announced the establishment of the scheme, "is one of great magnitude. Its development will result in a very great and rapid increase in the number of training schools, already large, and achieve an increased output of first-line pilots, observers, and air gunners which, combined with our home effort, will ensure that the greatly increased requirements in trained *personnel* are fully met. The aim, in short, is to achieve by co-operative effort Air Forces of overwhelming strength." In his broadcast address on 11th October, Mr. Menzies referred to the scheme as "the most spectacular and most decisive joint effort of the British nations in this war."

Mr. Menzies gave an outline of the scheme in his broadcast, as did also Mr. Mackenzie King in a statement issued in Ottawa on the same date. Sir Kingsley Wood had already explained its main features in the House of Commons on 10th October. It embraced both the training of pilots and other *personnel* of air crews for the home and Dominion air forces on a co-operative basis, and also the expansion of the production of aircraft in the Dominions participating in it. Training schools were to be established in Canada, Australia and New Zealand, to supplement the existing schools, and in Canada the *personnel* thus trained would receive their final course. A proportion of the young men passing out of the elementary flying schools in the United Kingdom would also proceed to Canada for their advanced training. The graduates of the Canadian school would join either Air Force squadrons maintained by their Dominions in the theatre of war, or else the

HANDLEY-PAGE
HAMPDEN

As powerful and
effective as it is
unusual in design.

(*Photo: Charles E,
Brown, London*)

BOMBING UP

Australian aircraft mechanics loading a bomb on the rack.

(Australian Official Photograph)

Royal Air Force ; those who had gone from Great Britain to Canada for their final course would return to the Royal Air Force in the field.

AUSTRALIA AND NEW ZEALAND

It was found at a later stage that greater facilities for complete training could be provided in Australia and New Zealand than had at first been contemplated, and the original proposals were modified slightly in this respect. The great majority of the trainees in Canada, said Mr. Mackenzie King, in a broadcast at Ottawa on 17th December, would be Canadians ; one-fifth would come from Australia and New Zealand, and some from Great Britain, Newfoundland and elsewhere for their advanced training. He stated that sixty-seven training schools, with staffs numbering nearly forty thousand, would be established in Canada, to teach flying, air observation, bombing, gunnery, air navigation and wireless operation, while about sixty new aerodromes would be built and twenty others enlarged. Most of the aircraft and engine spare parts would be contributed by Great Britain, but a number of machines for elementary training would be ordered in Canada. The cost of the scheme over a period of about three years would be about $600,000,000, and of this Canada's share would be $350,000,000. The Canadian schools will turn out yearly about seven thousand pilots, and twelve thousand observers, gunners, navigators and wireless operators.

Australia's expenditure under the scheme during the same period, Mr. Menzies stated on 15th December,

1939, and 29th February, 1940, was expected to be £A.50,000,000 ; this will include the cost of thirty-six new training schools. Her contribution in terms of *personnel* will be over fourteen thousand pilots and over sixteen thousand observers, gunners and wireless operators. A few thousand of these will be trained finally in Canada and all the rest in Australia. For training in Australia a ground staff of twenty-seven thousand would be needed. The intake of recruits in that country will be about one thousand a month, when the recruiting campaign, which has been organised by Sir Donald Cameron, is in full swing. In all, it is expected that 250,000 applicants will be interviewed in two and a half years, and of these some fifty thousand will be selected. Three thousand machines will be needed, including one thousand large service machines for advanced training which are being lent by Great Britain. These, according to a statement made by Mr. Fairbairn on 18th February, will include three to four hundred Fairey Battles and five hundred Avro Ansons. Large schools for technical training—in tool-making, electricians' and wireless operators' duties, are also to be formed. The maximum rate of output in Australia, it was stated by Mr. J. V. Fairbairn, the Minister for Air, on 9th January, would be reached at the beginning of 1942 and maintained throughout 1942–43. New Zealand's part in the scheme is also a noteworthy one, though naturally (in view of the smaller population) on a less ambitious scale than Australia's. Her contribution will be nearly ten thousand pilots, observers and gunners, and the total cost to her during three years is estimated at something approaching £20,000,000. In each year nine hundred airmen are to be fully trained in New Zealand itself, Mr. Jones, the Minister for Defence, stated on 18th March, 1940, and some two thousand more will receive initial training there and then go to Canada for their completing course.

Missions from Australia and New Zealand were dispatched to Ottawa in October, as was also one from the United Kingdom, headed by Lord Riverdale and including a number of Air Ministry officials. Captain Harold Balfour, the Under-Secretary of State for Air, visited Ottawa a little later in connection with the scheme. The annual output of trainees aimed at was stated at that time by Lord Riverdale to be in the neighbourhood of thirty thousand.[1] This figure is a clear addition to the very large number who will be fully trained in Great Britain and also in South Africa and India, neither of which countries is participating in the scheme, though both will largely expand their training facilities. So will Southern Rhodesia, which will train volunteers from the Rhodesias and other African colonies, as well as a number of young men from Great Britain, at seven training schools (three elementary, three senior, one observers').

The German break-through in France in May, 1940, affected the progress of the air-training scheme in several ways. The immediate result was that Britain, needing now all her available aircraft and trained airmen for her own defence, was unable to assist to the extent contemplated in the original plan. The Dominions were obliged, therefore, to shoulder a greater load of responsibility for the supply both of

---

[1] Compare our own " typical pre-expansion entry of approximately 300 pilots and 1,600 airmen a year." (*Statement relating to Defence*, issued 2nd March, 1938).

aeronautical equipment and of flying and other instructional staff. They rose to the occasion and succeeded in organising other sources of supply in a short time, with the result that not only was the scheme saved from collapse but the programmes were accelerated.

In the last great war Canada was found to be in many respects an ideal country in which to train young airmen, and the other Dominions have also various natural advantages in this respect. No. 4 School of Military Aeronautics was established in Canada in 1917, and became a very important contributory to the manning of the Royal Flying Corps in the later stages of the war. To-day the arguments for concentrating flying instruction and aircraft manufacture as far as possible in the overseas Empire are stronger still. The increased speed and range of modern bombers make it advisable, as already stated, that there should be available a number of establishments of both these kinds well beyond the reach of European attack. In the Dominions, moreover, there is plenty of elbow room for the flying man and the climatic conditions are on the whole more favourable for intensive instruction than in these islands. As regards Canada, in particular, the huge resources of the United States are within easy reach.

U.S.A.

Those resources would become of vital importance if it should be found that production in Great Britain itself were rendered difficult as a result of air raids at a later stage of the war. In any event they will constitute a valuable addition to the resources of Great

AUSTRALIAN AIRMEN

Pilots of the Coastal Command who take
their part in the defence of Britain's coasts.

(Official Photograph

BRISTOL
BEAUFORT
BOMBER

A new medium
bomber of outstand-
ing performance.

(Photo: *Charles E.
Brown, London*)

Britain and the Dominions. Already we have obtained a considerable number of Harvard Trainers and Lockheed Hudson reconnaissance aircraft from the United States. The latter have done good service in the Coastal Command. France had found the Curtiss P.36 fighters a useful auxiliary to her own Moranes. She had also obtained a number of Martin 167 and Douglas DB-7 bombers from America ; we are obtaining various machines from the same source. It is a comforting thought that the magnificent designing ability and manufacturing plants over there are at Britain's service, and that the United States Government has authorised the sale to us of their latest types, which are unsurpassed in the world. Our main source of supply, however, must be Britain itself, with the Dominions ; anything we draw from the United States will be only in the nature of an " extra " to our own production. But, so long as we have the money to pay for the American machines and the ships to carry them—or enough ferry pilots to take them over the Canadian frontiers and the petrol then to fly them to Botwood and thence to this country—we shall be able to rely on a most useful addition to our own immense production from that quarter.

The main benefit which we shall reap from the Empire air scheme will be the human rather than the material crop. A magnificent body of young airmen, fully trained, will be its first-fruits. The congestion in the flying schools at home will be relieved and training in this country will be facilitated as a result. The problem of the manning of the squadrons of this country and the Dominions will be solved. How many pilots, observers, gunners and wireless operators will be available when the scheme is at its peak has not been disclosed, but it will certainly be an immense number. Moreover, the air crews produced under the British scheme will be, it can confidently be asserted, the finest material trained to the last ounce : men of a race which has fully proved that in the air, as at sea and on land, its fighting spirit is unsurpassed by any nation in the world.

In a speech delivered on 31st January, 1940, Mr. Chamberlain described the Empire scheme as an effort by the Dominions " to canalise and concentrate their forces in order to forge a mighty weapon of war." It will, indeed, be a mighty weapon, of the most finely tempered steel. How and where it will carve its way to victory cannot yet be known. What can be foretold with assurance is that it will not fail in the hands of those who wield it.

CHAPTER 4

THE SPLENDID MACHINES

" THE BEST IN THE WORLD "

GREAT numbers of machines and men would be of little avail in war if the machines were " duds " and the men laggards in fight or poorly trained. The quality of the human and material elements of air power is of the first importance. If it is not high, then vaunted air power is a sham and a pretence. How do we stand in these respects ? It is a question which has to be considered not, as it were, *in vacuo* and absolutely, but relatively and with regard always to the *matériel* and *personnel* of other air services. The standard of comparison is necessarily an objective one.

At present there is little doubt that we have an advantage in quality of *matériel*. " The war in the air has not only demonstrated the indomitable courage of British pilots," said Sir Kingsley Wood at Bristol on 10th February, 1940, " but the definite technical superiority or power of many of our machines. Before the war much had been done by long and patient work in increasing the power and efficiency of our machines. The Hurricane and the Spitfire to-day carry twice as many guns as their predecessors, while the policy of fitting our bombers with power-driven turrets has represented a revolution in the design of military aircraft. Our eight-gun fighters have acquitted themselves magnificently, and we believe them to be the best machines of their kind in the world."

" High quality," Sir Kingsley Wood went on, " has always been the constant policy of the British Air Ministry ; it has certainly paid and we do not intend to forgo it. Since the outbreak of war we have been steadily increasing our strength and perfecting our air defences. New squadrons have been formed, and the improving and rearming of others have been going on continually." The war, he pointed out, was being fought in the design departments and on the drawing boards as well as in the factories and in the air. " Development and advance must be our watchwords." We must go on " perfecting present types and introducing others with even higher speed, longer range and better armament." Fortunate, indeed, it is for us that no nation in the world has a longer tradition or a higher standard in engineering.

Sir Kingsley Wood's reminder of the need for increasing development and improvement is particularly timely ; it shows that we shall not regard our present superiority in performance as satisfying all the needs of the situation. That superiority is, in fact, an incentive to achieve something better. A technical journal has put the matter in its true perspective.

" When a certain type has proved its tactical superiority there is a tendency to believe that it will continue to hold its advantage. That tendency is all the more understandable when production of that type is in full swing after months of preparation. But the enemy is constantly improving his aeroplanes all the more earnestly under the spur of technical inferiority. . . . We must maintain the superiority of fighting power as well as merely increasing numbers. Three of the best aeroplanes in the world are worth more compared with ten which are out-flown and out-fought by the enemy. We have the best aeroplanes now. There is no reason why we should not have the best aeroplanes—but different aeroplanes—a year hence, as well as more of them than the enemy."[1]

The counsel is wise and salutary. No apology is needed for drawing attention at the opening of this chapter to the supreme importance of avoiding anything in the nature of complacency and self-satisfaction because we happen for the time to have better aircraft than our enemy has. That position is not stereotyped. It may change to our disadvantage. There are ups and downs in the game of capping your enemy's performance in the air. We learnt that lesson in 1914–18.

THE BATTLE OF DESIGNS

We began that war with a good machine, for its day— the B.E.2C. It held its own until the Fokker mono-plane, with synchronised gear for its machine-gun, appeared and practically drove our B.E.2C's out of the sky. We tried to redress the balance with various machines—the D.H.2, the F.E.8, the F.E.2B, the Sopwith " 1½ strutter "—but it was the French Nieuport

[1] *The Aeroplane*, 9th February, 1940.

which mastered the Fokker E.1. Then came the Halberstadt and Albatros biplanes and others of the famous "D" series. They were better than our fighters at that time; we suffered grave losses in the spring of 1917. We did not despair. We retorted with the Sopwith "Camel" and the S.E.5, a little later with the Sopwith "Snipe" and the S.E.5A, and in 1918 we had the mastery in the air. The famous Fokker D.VII biplane was a hard machine to master, but we had the whip hand of it. That was largely because there were no engines to equal our Rolls-Royce and Bentley Rotary. It was a question of the drawing-office, the design staff, the engineering workshop, and we won in each.

There will probably be a similar see-saw process in the struggle for supremacy in the air in the present war. One side may have the upper hand at one moment and the other at the next. The oscillation may not be so frequent or violent as it was in the last war. That, at least, is the opinion of a well-known technical authority, Mr. A. H. R. Fedden, the chief designer of the Aero Engine Department of the Bristol Aeroplane Company. He has written:

"Discrepancies between opposing aircraft were the main causes of the ebb and flow of air supremacy during the last war. Such wide variations are not so likely to occur in the present conflagration, as the basic principles of design are too well understood and diffused for large differences to be expected. Further, the introduction of the all-metal stressed-skin aircraft necessitates extensive tooling and equipment. These facts, combined with the much larger quantities, have necessitated the freezing of design of both aircraft and engines for much longer periods."[1]

We were fortunate in one respect in having begun to re-arm only when we did. If we had begun to re-arm on the same scale in 1934 or 1935 we should have filled up the squadrons with Harts, Hinds, Furies, Glosters—obsolescent biplanes, of much lower performance than the low-winged, clean monoplanes that were about to supersede them. In 1936 the Blenheims, Battles, Spitfires and Hurricanes were ready to go into production. We began our big re-equipment, it can be seen now, just at the right time. The result was that we were on top in performance in the autumn of 1939 ; we have the most *up-to-date* air force in the world.

For that result we owe a debt of gratitude to the designers who were responsible initially for these fine machines—to B. N. Wallis, Sydney Camm, the late R. J. Mitchell and F. S. Barnwell, and others. Not sufficient credit has been given to the design staffs of the great aircraft firms, yet without their constant and devoted efforts to improve upon existing types we could not hope to win the race for higher performance. Other and better machines will replace those which are now in use, but here again we may hope that, thanks to the designers and the constructors and the very able staffs of the Directorates of the Air Ministry concerned with research and development, we shall not be left behind.

We may expect, indeed, to have something better

[1] Paper in *Flight*, 14th December, 1939.

than the Wellington in the air before this war is ended ; and the Wellington is the finest heavy bomber which any nation has in service at present. It is the younger but bigger brother of the Wellesley, which set up a record by the flight from Egypt to Australia on 5th–7th November, 1938. The two Wellesleys which made their first landing at Darwin after leaving Ismailia covered 7,162 miles in their non-stop flight. The third, which alighted at Koepang to refuel, had covered 6,600 miles before landing there, and this in itself was a record, promptly to be superseded by the achievement of its two comrades. The average speed for the flight was about 150 miles per hour. The Wellington, like the Wellesley, is built on the geodetic principle, that is, more or less as a basket is built. The curved metal framework, of contoured duralumin bars, requires no large cross-bracing members internally, and hence there is plenty of room available for useful load inside the fuselage and wings. A heavy load of fuel, bombs and military equipment can be carried, as well as the machine-guns mounted in the Frazer-Nash power-driven turrets, located in nose and tail, affording protection to front and rear. With its two Pegasus XVIII engines of 980 horse power each the Wellington has a range of 3,240 miles and a maximum speed of about 260 miles per hour. The performance with two Hercules sleeve-valve engines of 1,375 horse power each, or with two Merlin engines of 1,075 horse power each, must be substantially better.

SPITFIRES

A flight of the famous Supermarine Spitfire Fighters which have taken such a heavy toll of German planes.

(Photo: Charles E. Brown, London)

VICKERS
WELLESLEY
BOMBER

Aircraft of this type hold the world's distance record, having flown non-stop from Egypt to Australia.

(Photo: Charles E. Brown, London)

THE BOMBERS

The French Air Army is now, alas ! out of the fight, but it is still of interest to note that the speed of the Wellington with Pegasus engines is apparently less than that of the (Lioré et Olivier) LeO 45, which can take either two Gnome-Rhone or two Hispano-Suiza engines, the horse power of the former being 1,050 and of the latter 1,100. The range of the French bomber (1,600 miles) is, however, only about half that of the Wellington. So, too, is the range of the Amiot 350, another heavy bomber which, again, can take either two Hispano-Suiza or two Gnome-Rhone engines. (The Amiot 370 is said to have a range of 4,000 miles.) Of the Italian bombers the Caproni Ca 135 and the Fiat Br 20 have ranges of 1,860 and 1,550 miles and top speeds of 273 and 268 miles per hour, respectively. The Savoia-Marchetti 79, now an old design, is still the most usual bomber ; its top speed is 270 miles per hour, and range about 1,600 miles. The range of the latest (American) Boeing " Flying Fortress," the largest bomber in the world, is as great as the Wellington's, and its bomb-load heavier, but then it is a four-engined bomber (Wright Cyclones of 1,000 horse power each) and hardly comparable. That is true also of the latest type of (American) Douglas bomber, for which a range of 3,000 miles and a bomb-load of 10,000 lbs. are claimed. The Douglas is a six-engined bomber. Relatively, the known performance of the Wellington, with its two engines, is superior to that of either of the American bombers.

The corresponding German bomber is the Heinkel

He 111K.V. With its two Junkers Jumo engines of 1,200 horse power at the take-off and 1,050 horse power at 4,200 metres' altitude, it has a range of 2,640 miles and a top speed of 274 miles per hour. The Heinkel, however, has only three machine-guns, as compared with the Wellington's six, and has no power-actuated gun turrets. The Heinkel which was brought down in Scotland in October, 1939, was carefully examined by experts, and the verdict was that it was inferior in most respects to the Wellington. It had two advantages only—the construction of its bullet-proof tanks and its direct petrol-injection system. The structural design and construction, said the report, were sound, the materials were excellent and the finish was good, but the location and power of the armament were poor and not to be compared with that of our own bombers of equivalent size. " There is no doubt that the Wellington is far more efficient as a fighting machine and capable of giving a much better account of itself against enemy fighters. Taken all round, the Wellington is the much better aeroplane, with greater range, defence and bomb-load achieved on less power, with only slightly less speed."[1]

As regards the petrol-injection system of the German machine, this is undoubtedly an advantage in so far as it eliminates the danger of ice-formation on the carburetters. It allows, moreover, a petrol of lower octane number—87—to be used in the German machines than in ours (octane number 100). On the whole, there is little to choose between the two systems. " A well-known American engineer, when asked for his ideas on the benefits of fuel injection as compared

[1] *The Aeroplane*, 5th January, 1940.

with the carburetter, stated that if the aero-engine, as developed, incorporated fuel injection instead of a carburetter, there would have been people just as anxious to fit the carburetter as they are apparently anxious to adopt fuel injection."[1]

The French Potez 63 is more or less the counterpart of the British Blenheim in the reconnaissance-bomber-fighter class. It was used extensively on the western front in this war. It is a low-wing monoplane with two Hispano-Suiza engines, or, alternatively, two Gnome-Rhone engines, carries two Hispano *canons* under the nose and also one or more machine-guns. It can be used as a twin-engined fighter as well as for reconnaissance. It is a rather short-range machine and in this respect not comparable to the Blenheim, especially the " long-nosed " variety. The medium bombers obtained by the French air force from America, the Martin 167 and the Douglas D.B.7, have a longer range (that of the Martin is 2,500 miles) and are faster than the Potez; indeed, the Douglas, which has two Pratt and Whitney twin Wasp engines, is claimed by the American Press to be the fastest bomber in the world. That is a disputable claim, and in any case neither of these American bombers appears to have as good an all-round performance as the Blenheim or its derivative, the Beaufort.

The German reconnaissance-bombers corresponding to the British " short " and " long-nosed " Blenheims are the Dornier Do 17 and 215, respectively. The former, commonly known as the " flying pencil," has the disadvantage of being cramped for space for its crew of three, who are huddled together forward of

[1] Article on " Aircraft Power Plants " in *Flight*, 8th February, 1940.

the wing, the bombs filling the fuselage aft of the front spar. The rear gun-turret is just aft of the pilot and the field of fire is much more restricted than in the Blenheim, in which the rear turret is further back. The Blenheim has, moreover, more room for the crew.[1] Compared with the latter the Do 17 is not a good fighting machine, its defence is poor, and it is not fast enough, even with Daimler-Benz 1,050 horse power engines, to escape from fighters.[2] The speed of the Blenheim IV, with Bristol Mercury XV engines of 920 horse power, is 295 miles per hour. The Do 215 is said to attain a speed of 392 miles per hour, but this would be possible only for a very restricted range. For long flights the speed would be about 250 miles per hour. It has more space for the crew than the Do 17 but carries only three machine-guns as compared with the five of the long-nosed Blenheim, which has four under the nose, firing forward, and one in a turret, to protect the rear. The Blenheim IV is classed, indeed, as a long-range fighter, and that it can hold its own even with the Messerschmitt Me 110 is evident from the result of the encounters which have taken place between them. It is undoubtedly a much more unpleasant machine to meet than the Do 215.

The Junkers Ju 87 dive-bomber was the machine principally used by the Germans in their spectacular drive through northern France. It is a single-engined bomber (Junkers Jumo 1,200 horse power), has two seats and three machine-guns, and carries only a moderate bomb load. It has no great range and is therefore unsuitable for deep raiding though formidable

[1] B. S. Shenstone, in *Aeronautics*, August, 1939, pp. 32, 33.
[2] *The Aeroplane*, 22nd December, 1939.

A VICKERS
WELLINGTON
BOMBER

This, the bigger
brother of the Wel-
lesley, has been very
largely used for our
long distance raids.

(Photo:
Barratt's Photo Press
Ltd., London)

BRISTOL
BLENHEIM
IN FLIGHT
Note the power-operated gun turret amidships.

(Photo:
Photopress Ltd.
London)

in tactical work in a battle zone. It is very vulnerable to fighter attack and many hundreds were destroyed by British fighters in France.

THE FIGHTERS

Of the four bombers which were shot down into the sea off the Firth of Forth on 16th October, 1939, two were reported to have been Do 215's, the other two being Heinkel He 111K's.[1] Recently the Germans have been making increasing use, especially for raids against shipping, of Junkers Ju 88 bombers. The Ju 88 was designed for three gun-positions, in the nose and above and below the fuselage. The two guns in the nose may be shell-firing. It has no tail gun. Carrying nearly two tons' load it has attained a speed of 321 miles an hour, over a course of 621 miles. At 300 miles an hour its range is over 1,200 miles, and with full military load its speed is understood to be 265 miles an hour and its range about 1,300 miles. It is evidently a formidable machine but would be completely outclassed, for speed, by our Spitfires, the latest versions of which are believed to have a top speed of over 400 miles per hour. Even the present Spitfire has been dived at over 600 miles per hour. A speed on the level of over 400 miles an hour is claimed for the two new American fighters, the Curtiss P.40 and the Bell Airacobra. The former is a development of the Curtiss Hawk, which was the P.36, and it has been reported that supplies of it, under the name Curtiss Hawk 81A, have been made available for the Allies. The Bell Airacobra is a fighter, originally

[1] *The Aeroplane*, 26th October, 1939.

known as the P.39, of novel design ; its power plant is an Allison engine and it carries a 37 mm. shell-firing gun in the nose, as well as four machine-guns. It appears, however, to be a rather " freakish " machine in some respects ; *inter alia*, it has the engine behind the pilot, who is thus deprived of the protection usually afforded by its bulk in the normal manœuvre of attack by a fighter.

The Spitfire is at present the star performer among British fighters, with the Hurricane a close rival. The corresponding fighter machines used by the French before their collapse were the Curtiss Hawk 75A and the Morane-Saulnier 406C. The Curtiss, which has a 900 horse power Pratt and Whitney engine and carries six machine-guns (two more than the original American fighter), won a great reputation by its success on 9th December, 1939. On that day there was an engagement between 9 Curtiss machines and 27 Messerschmitts (apparently Me 109's) and 9 of the latter were brought down without the loss of a single French machine. The Morane fighter has been less successful, but has had its victories too. Its armament is different from that of the Curtiss ; it has a 20 mm. *canon* firing through the airscrew and two machine-guns in the wings. Its engine is a Hispano-Suiza of 860 horse power. Its speed is about 300 miles an hour—roughly the same as that of the Curtiss Hawk. Two other French fighters, the Bloch 151 and the Dewoitine D.520, have a higher speed but had not come into general use in *l'Armée de l'Air*. The Italian fighter Macchi C.200 has a maximum speed of 313 miles per hour ; the Fiat G.50 is about 8 miles per hour slower ; each machine has two large-bore machine-guns.

The corresponding German fighters are the Messerschmitt Me 109 and 110[1] and the Heinkel He 113.

The Me 110 is undoubtedly a more formidable machine than the Me 109. The latter has some unsatisfactory characteristics. A Messerschmitt 109 which the French captured intact was crashed before its performance could be tested against that of the British fighters. It was tried against the Curtiss and Morane fighters, by which the French pilots found it to be distinctly outclassed ; it was much less manœuvrable, was inclined to develop wing and aileron flutter, and had a rather high stalling speed. It was not considered to be a good machine for night work.[2] Mr. Sydney Camm, the designer of the Hurricane, has expressed the view that the Messerschmitt is " not a clean aircraft," having too many " excrescences," and that the method adopted in it of retracting the undercarriage is a " very inferior job." It is liable, he states, to a partial stall on a high-speed turn, and so can be evaded by our medium bombers.[3] The Me 110 is also unsatisfactory in some respects, e.g., in having neither a bullet-proof windscreen nor armour-plated protection for the pilot.[4]

In the House of Commons on 10th October, 1939, Sir Kingsley Wood said : " The plain facts seem to be that our latest fighters are definitely better than their German counterparts." Referring again to our fighters

[1] The Messerschmitts, being made at the Bayerische Flugzeug-werke A.G., Augsberg, are sometimes called the Bf109 and Bf110. Professor Willi Messerschmitt was the designer.

[2] These particulars of the trial were given by Major C. C. Turner in the *Daily Telegraph*, 5th December, 1939.

[3] Quoted in *Flight*, 14th December, 1939.

[4] Statement by Lord Beaverbrook, Minister for Aircraft Production, in broadcast, 24th July, 1940.

on 12th December, he said : " Not only have they twice the gun-power of the Messerschmitt but they have markedly better flying characteristics and are superior both in control and manœuvrability at high speeds." " All our types—the Hurricane, the Spitfire, and the new Defiant—and all our pilots," said Mr. Churchill in the House of Commons on 4th June, 1940, " have been vindicated as superior to what they have at present to face."

The Me 110 is a long-range fighter and was intended, there is reason to suppose, for escort work. It has a fuel tankage capacity of 400 gallons and a range of 1,500 miles. Whether its armament makes it a suitable machine for escorting bombers is, however, open to question. Its main armament is fixed, consisting of two 20 mm. shell-firing guns in the nose, as well as two machine-guns in the wings, all firing forward, with one or two movable machine-guns aft. To bring its full fire-power to bear upon an attacking fighter it would have to turn away from the escorted bombers and leave them for the time uncovered. It might indeed lose touch with them altogether in a prolonged encounter, in which case they would be at the mercy of the interceptors. A fighter such as our Boulton and Paul " Defiant," which has a battery of four machine-guns in a power-driven turret amidships, would be in a better position to protect its convoy of bombers without leaving them open to attack.

Another German fighter, which was not seen in action until 22nd April, 1940, when one was encountered and damaged by a Hurricane on the western front, is the Heinkel He 112, a single seater with a Daimler-Benz DB 601 engine of 1,150 horse power. It is reported

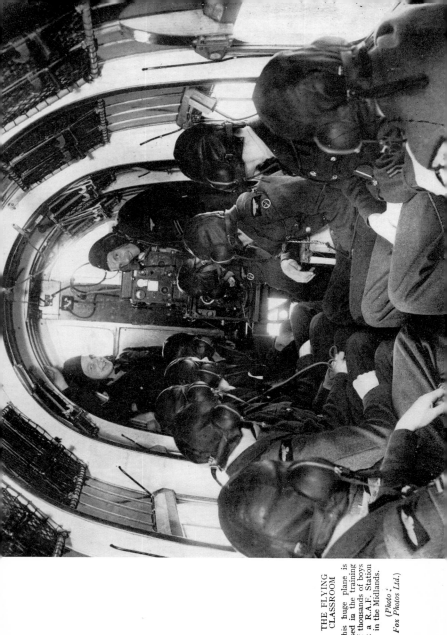

THE FLYING
CLASSROOM
This huge plane is
used in the training
of thousands of boys
at a R.A.F. Station
in the Midlands.

(Photo :
Fox Photos Ltd.)

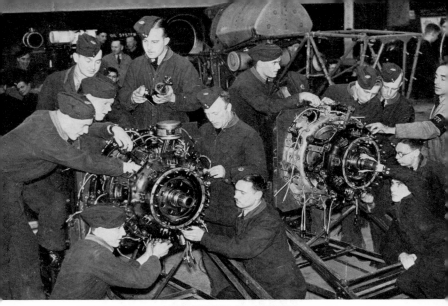

AIRCRAFTMEN IN TRAINING
At this technical school in the Midlands recruits are trained as flight mechanics, engineers, fitters, etc.
(*Official Photograph*)

APPRENTICES UNDER INSTRUCTION
Here is a class learning to carry out repairs to fuselages and wings.
(*Photo: London News Agency Ltd.*)

to have two machine-guns in the nose and two more in the wings, with a shell-gun firing through the hub of the airscrew, and its speed is stated to be about 360 miles per hour. Its range is apparently short—certainly much shorter than that of the two-engined Me 110—but it can apparently, be fitted with extra tanks ; in that case, however, its general performance would be somewhat reduced. There is some reason to believe that the He 112 has not been considered altogether a success and that its place will be taken by the He 113, which is already in full-scale production. It has been reported, indeed, that a He 113 was encountered at an early stage in the war, but the identification was probably wrong. It is a small single-seater fighter with a 1,500 horse-power Daimler-Benz and a reputed top speed of 400 miles per hour ; its armament is said to be a cannon and two machine-guns. He 113's were first encountered on 20th July over Germany, when our bombers damaged one of them ; others were met over the English Channel later in the month. The other and newer fighter is the Focke-Wulf FW 187, a two-seater with two DB 601 engines ; it is stated to carry either six machine-guns or four machine-guns and two shell-firing guns, as well as one free gun. Its speed is also about 360 miles per hour and it is credited with a remarkable rate of climb. Neither type is as formidable a fighter as some new types which we have not brought out of the bag as yet.

Yet another and still later German fighter, the FW 198, has been spoken of and may be meant as a surprise packet when heavy fighting in the air develops. It is remarkable in having two fuselages and a " pusher " engine (Daimler-Benz DB 601) and is supposed to have a speed of about 400 miles per hour. Not having the airscrew in front of him the pilot can be provided with a ring of machine-guns in the nose, and this is said to enable a cone of fire to be directed at the target with more destructive effect than when the guns are located in the wings; the claim is doubtful and in any case the FW 198 is probably not as good a fighter machine as our own latest models.[1]

ARMOUR AND GUNS

It is evident that the aircraft equipment of all the belligerents is in a transitional state at present. It has been undergoing a process of testing by trial and error, and the need for modification and improvements in various respects has been demonstrated. Already it is known, for instance, that the German bombers have been provided with better protection for their gunners. The armament of a bomber is seen to be of more importance than the experience of the civil war in Spain was thought to have indicated. Then, it was considered, prematurely, as now appears, that speed was the best safeguard of the bomber. Whether, as an answer to the improved armament of the bomber, the shell-firing gun will replace the battery of machine-guns as the main armament of the fighter remains to be seen. Certainly the multiple machine-guns of the fighters seem in all conscience to be sufficiently effective. The volume of machine-gun fire of a whole infantry brigade in 1914 it has been pointed out, was only half that of a

[1] Particulars of the FW 198 are given in *The Aeroplane* of 1st March, 1940.

single Spitfire or Hurricane.[1] Of the Heinkel He 111K which was brought down near Dalkeith in Scotland on 28th October, an eye-witness wrote at the time : "Every part of the German aircraft bore traces of devastating machine-gun fire ; even the two metal propellers were drilled with holes."[2] "When a German machine has come up against them," said Air Chief Marshal Sir Cyril Newall on 13th December, 1939, in an interview in France, referring to our Hurricanes and Spitfires, "it has invariably finished up looking like a colander." Whether the long range of the shell-firing gun will give it an advantage over the much quicker fire and greater volume of fire of the machine-gun battery will be proved, no doubt, before the war is much older. It is possible that the shifting platform of the cannon and the immense speeds at which air combats are fought to-day will be found to favour the smaller gun in practice. A hit from a shell is, of course, more destructive—if a hit is obtained—but the odds against a lucky shot are much greater, simply because the cannon has a slower rate of fire.

FIGHTER VERSUS BOMBER

It is possible, nevertheless, that a tendency may be seen towards the building of bigger fighters, of the two-engined type, with a heavier content of armament, ammunition and petrol. This may come about for a variety of reasons. The larger fighter will be found necessary, perhaps, because the bomber with its

[1] Air Commodore P. F. M. Fellowes in *The Army Quarterly*, January, 1940, p. 270.
[2] *The Times*, 30th October, 1939.

self-sealing petrol tanks and its armoured protection for the crew may become almost immune from successful assault by guns of small calibre. There is the further reason that with the immense speed of discharge of the machine-gun of the Browning type, all the fighter's ammunition may be expended in a few bursts of fire and then it may find itself exposed to destruction by enemy interceptors, perhaps far from its own lines and without hope of rescue. The machine which can carry plenty of ammunition would be less liable to suffer such a fate ; and if fighters of larger size are built, the opportunity may be taken to give them the benefit of a shell-firing gun of Oerlikon, Madsen or other type, in addition to machine-guns. That seems, indeed, to be already the tendency in Germany, and the fact that we, too, are bringing shell-guns into service is not without considerable significance.[1]

The bomber, on the other hand, may well decrease in size. The heavy bomber, especially the biggest type, with four engines, is too easy a target for fighters, and too slow in evasive action when under fire from anti-aircraft artillery, to be as effective an instrument for conveying a given weight of explosive or incendiary bombs to a given point and depositing it there as a number of smaller, lighter and faster bombers, carrying altogether an equivalent load. The result may well be that the bomber and the fighter will tend to approximate to one another in size and that the one class will overlap the other. This tendency is to be seen already

[1] In a speech at Margate on 21st March, 1940, Captain Harold Balfour, Under-Secretary of State for Air, said : "Not only are our cannon-guns in full swing of production in this country, but our fighters equipped with them have already contributed to the destruction of some of the enemy machines."

in our own Blenheims, which can be used alternatively as bomber-reconnaissance or as fighter machines. All such speculations are, however, more or less guess-work at present. There may be a good many surprising changes in aeronautical equipment before the war is ended.

Meanwhile, it is ground for satisfaction that, so far at least, British aircraft have no reason to fear comparison with any other country's equipment. If only the present lead can be maintained, and if our production increases, as there is every reason to expect that it will, all will be well. There is in fact no reason why the Royal Air Force should not be able to repeat its triumph of the last war and to emerge from that struggle predominant both quantitatively and qualitatively. We have not disclosed the full contents of our splendid armoury of the air as yet.

CHAPTER 5

THE MEN OF THE AIR

AIRMANSHIP WINS

"SUPERIOR seamanship won our sea fights," said Lord Chatfield, Minister for the Co-ordination of Defence, at Cardiff on 17th February, 1940, "and so also it will be the relative airmanship that will decide war in the air. Every act of airmanship in this war gives me confidence that in the fight for the command of the air, whenever it commences on a great scale, our most gallant airmen will prove superior."

The most splendid equipment will not avail if the man using it is found wanting. The man in the aircraft counts as much as the machine, or more. It is on his skill, determination, fighting spirit, "guts," that the issue of a combat hangs. The quality of the airman is as vital a factor in air warfare as the quality of the aircraft, and quality is not simply the innate courage and physical and mental hardihood which men owe "to skies that knit their heartstrings right, to fields that bred them brave." There must be professional proficiency as well as valour, and that is a matter of long training. Training cannot be skimped in the flying arm.

Not only a host of competent instructors but an

army of ground workers, too, is needed to keep an air force effective. The men below the aircraft are hardly less important than the men in them. It is their job to groom the machine, to keep it fit for its work, to see that it is tuned up to battle pitch. On their work depends the due functioning of the machine in the air. If they are slack or negligent, if their care of the equipment for which they are responsible is not unremitting and highly competent, they may let the pilot down, literally as well as metaphorically.

R.A.F.

The Royal Air Force is fortunate in these respects. Its human material is good to start with, and it is highly trained ; perhaps the most highly trained in the world. Both the air crews and the ground staff are thoroughly instructed. The importance as well as the growth of the ground staff of the Royal Air Force was reflected in the splitting up in May, 1940, of the Training Command into two distinct Commands—Flying Training and Technical Training—each under an Air Marshal. There is nothing shoddy or makeshift about the system under which the *personnel*, flying and non-flying alike, is produced. Both the airmen and the mechanics have to pass a gruelling test before they take their places in the army of the air—an army now greater than our whole army proper of a few years ago.

The flying *personnel* is composed partly of officers, partly of non-commissioned officers and aircraftmen. The officers are normally found in two different ways. First, there are those who are trained at the Royal Air Force College, Cranwell—the Sandhurst of the

Royal Air Force. Here the course is of two years' duration and the entrants come mainly from the public schools, but a certain number of aircraft apprentices (see later) are also admitted each year. These Cranwell cadets produce the main body of the permanent officers of the Air Force. Then there are the short-service officers, who serve for four years with the regular Air Force, then passing to the Reserve for six years (which period is extensible) with a liability to rejoin for service in an emergency. Shortly before the present war candidates were given the opportunity to serve for six years with the regular Air Force and four years in the Reserve, the gratuity of £300 payable at the end of the four years' active service being raised to £500 for those who served for six years. A few of these short-service officers are selected each year for permanent commissions. During the period in the Reserve officers are required to perform annual flying training. The Reserve was also manned in part by pilots already trained and engaged in civil flying, but the chief source has been that referred to above. Non-commissioned officers who had been pilots during their regular service were also passed to the Reserve, with corresponding liabilities.

R.A.F.V.R.

In 1936 the source of supply of the *personnel* of the Royal Air Force was substantially enlarged as the result of an important innovation. This was the formation of the Royal Air Force Volunteer Reserve. Arrangements were made for teaching a large number of young men to fly, at no cost to themselves, at a number of civil flying establishments throughout the

OPERATIONS
Operation Room at an R.A.F. Headquarters.
(*Official Photograph*)

THE LINK TRAINER
With the aid of this most ingenious device the budding airman
learns a great deal about flying without leaving the ground.
(*Photo : London News Agency Ltd.*)

MILES MASTER
Constructed of wood, with a Rolls-Royce Kestrel engine, the " Miles Master " is the
fastest training aircraft in the world. Large numbers are used by the R.A.F.
(Photo : Sport & General Press Agency Ltd.)

THE HARVARD
An American aircraft which is used by the R.A.F. for advanced training.
(Photo : Keystone Press Agency Ltd.)

country. They were allowed to train in their spare time and at centres near their homes or places of employment. After a certain standard of proficiency was attained the volunteer pilot could be attached to a Royal Air Force unit for continuous training for a period up to six months in duration. At first the Volunteer Reserve was confined to a pilots' section, and as such proved itself a great success. When Sir Kingsley Wood made his speech on the Air Estimates on 9th March, 1939, he was able to announce that 2,500 pilots were under training in this Reserve alone. Flying training of Volunteer Reserve members was being carried out, he stated, at thirty-two centres, and the number would be increased to fifty during the year. The success of the pilots' section led to the formation of an air-crew section, for the training of air observers, air gunners and wireless operators. Sections were also formed for equipment officers and medical officers, and for technical " other ranks," such as fitters, carpenters, electricians, photographers, instrument repairers, equipment assistants, and motor drivers, as well as for ordinary aircraft hands. In addition, a Civilian Wireless Reserve was organised for the enrolment of men with a good working knowledge of telegraphy and Morse signalling.

It is of interest to note that the pilot who shot down the Heinkel bomber off the Firth of Forth on 27th February, 1940, was a young Volunteer Reserve officer ; he was taking part in his first Fighter Command patrol. The Heinkel had been attacked by two other fighters, but it was he who registered the kill. After he had given it a burst from his machine-guns both of the Heinkel's engines were seen to be ablaze, and it alighted on the sea, where its crew of four were rescued.

A.A.F.

Another, and much older, feeder of the Royal Air Force was the Auxiliary Air Force, formed early in the 'twenties, and corresponding more or less to the Territorial Army. Here, again, the amateur airmen were the flying *personnel*, but the Auxiliary Air Force differed from the Volunteer Reserve in that it was a force organised in squadrons, instantly ready to take their place in the system of air defence. There were twenty A.A.F. squadrons when the war began. Originally a force of bombing units, they had become fighter squadrons for the most part by 1939. They were highly efficient, as they showed most unmistakably on 16th October, 1939. On that day an A.A.F. squadron shot down three German bombers over the Firth of Forth. They "lost their amateur status" on that occasion, it was said. On 13th January, they scored again. Three pilots of an A.A.F. squadron—a timber merchant, a solicitor, and an auctioneer in civil life— attacked a Heinkel many thousands of feet above the Forth. Each of the three fired bursts before the enemy escaped into a cloud ; then he dived towards the sea, finally to be shot down by a regular pilot who had joined the combat. On 9th February the Auxiliaries scored again, shooting down a Heinkel in a field near North Berwick, and yet again on 22nd February, when they forced another to land near St. Abb's Head. For leading his squadron "with magnificent dash and courage" on these occasions, Squadron-Leader Andrew Douglas Farquhar was awarded the Distinguished Flying Cross. By early August, 1940, Auxiliary Air Force pilots had shot down over two hundred enemy aircraft.

The Auxiliary Air Force consititutes the non-regular element of the Royal Air Force. The regular element, so far as the flying *personnel* is concerned, is composed of two sub-elements—the permanent and the non-permanent. Flying is a young man's game (though there are plenty of exceptions to prove the rule), and it is essential that there should be in the air arm a high proportion of pilots who do not look to the service for a career for life. If it were not so the establishment would be top-heavy or, alternatively, the prospects of promotion would be hopeless. The difficulty is avoided under the system of short-service commissions, already referred to, which was introduced soon after the end of the last war. The entrants by this door are, at any given date, greatly superior in numbers to the entrants *viâ* Cranwell. The training is shorter but it is not less rigorous and thorough.

Airmen in the Making

Normally, the training of the entrant on a short-service commission comprised five stages. A couple of months were first spent at an Elementary and Reserve Flying School, that is, a civil training school which specialised in instructional courses for *ab initio* pupils and refresher courses for reserve pilots. After this the pupil went for a couple of weeks to the Royal Air Force Depot, for instruction in drill, discipline and the routine of the service. Thence he passed to a flying school conducted by the Royal Air Force itself, for a course of " intermediate " training, and it was at this stage that he became a military pilot, though still without his wings. Intermediate training lasted a little over three months, and was succeeded by a similar period in an " advanced " training squadron at the Flying Training School, where navigation and armament duties were taught as well as flying in the more advanced machines. During the last part of this period some weeks were spent at an armament training camp, for the practice of live bombing and machine-gun firing at coastal ranges. Since the war began the programme of training has been modified in some respects but it is not less comprehensive and thorough than it was before.

While direct commissioning was the practice in peace, the rule at present is to allow entry, for the " duration," into the general duties (flying) branch of the Royal Air Force only through the ranks, with certain specified exceptions. Entrants are enlisted in the Volunteer Reserve and commissions are granted only on completion of flying training or subsequently. The exceptions are confined to a few categories of men with special qualifications. Past or present members of University Air squadrons can be commissioned directly in the flying branch. So can experienced pilots at the age of twenty-eight to forty-eight who are suitable for employment on instructional or other flying of a non-operational nature. (The age limit for entry of candidates for operational duties is eighteen to twenty-eight). A limited number of direct commissions is also given to men of the age of twenty-eight to thirty-five who are considered suitable in view of their knowledge and experience of shooting for employment as commissioned air gunners. The administrative, equipment, accountant, legal, medical,

R.A.F. FIGHTER AIRCRAFT ON THE WESTERN FRONT
Giving an impression of what it looks like to be attacked by
Hurricanes : the fighters are seen pulling away after making contact.

AIRSPEED OXFORD
One of the types of aircraft used for training the R.A.F.
(*Photo : Charles E. Brown, London*)

THE
PHOTOGRAPH
SPEAKS

Photographs taken on
reconnaissance flights
are developed at
once and examined
by experts.

(Official Photograph)

dental and technical branches are also manned by direct commissioning.

The system of training in the flying branch is now as follows :—Men who are to be trained as pilots or observers go first to the Receiving Centre and then an Initial Training Wing to learn drill and undergo disciplinary instruction ; they are initiated here into the mysteries of the Link Trainer (see below). The Initial Training Wing serves as a pool for candidates for whom room cannot be found for the time in the flying schools. The candidate for *pilot's* duty then goes to an Elementary Flying Training School, where he learns to fly, and, this accomplished, passes to a Flying Training School, which is a Royal Air Force establishment, for courses in both intermediate and advanced flying. At the Flying Training School the pupil who is to be a fighter pilot receives instruction at first on the single-engined Harvard trainer (and the pupil earmarked for bombers on the twin-engined Oxford) and then on the Master I, which is the fastest training aircraft in the world and looks and feels like a fighter. From these machines the passage is easy to the advanced types. The pupil's next and final change is one to an operational training unit, where he gains experience of operational conditions, and is ready to take his place in a squadron. The *observer* pupil's training career is different. From the Initial Training Wing he passes to the Air Observer Navigation School, and having completed his course there, to a Bombing and Gunnery school. The embryo *wireless operator-gunner* follows yet a third line. He goes first to the Recruits' Receiving Centre for drill and disciplinary instruction, passes thence to the Electrical and Wireless School, and next to the Initial Training Wing, going finally to a Bombing and Gunnery School. Both the observer and the wireless operator-air gunner are given experience at operational training units in the same way as the pilot.

The *navigator's* training is also lengthy and very thorough. The pupil goes to the Receiving Centre and Initial Training Wing and, having mastered drill and discipline, he must then devote many months' hard work to learning air navigation. This accomplished, he has to spend a good many weeks learning bombing and gunnery, and finally to gain practical experience at an operational training unit. If he wants to obtain the highest qualification he must go on, after all this, to an air navigation school, to learn " astronomical navigation " and other abstruse subjects of the kind. The navigator's training, it should be added, does not include learning to fly an aircraft ; the pilot-navigator must complete two courses.

How thorough the training of the pilots of the Royal Air Force is may be seen from the fact that the young airman is by no means finished with " lessons " when he has won his wings and left the Flying Training School. If he is (for instance) to fly bombers, he must go on from the Flying Training School to the Bomber Command Training Group. So, also, must the observer and the wireless operator-air gunner. At the Training Group they have to undergo intensive training before they are considered ready to be admitted into operational or reserve squadrons. They have to attend lectures on airmanship, navigation, armament, signals, reconnaissance, photography, tactics and meteorology. They are taught log-keeping, map-reading and astronomical air navigation. The technique of evading as well as fighting tactics is studied. The young bombing airman has to learn all about reconnaissance, what sort of information he is required to bring back, how types of targets may be identified, how vulnerable points can be recognised, how photographs can best be obtained. He must know a great deal about the variations of wind with altitude, about ice-formation, about cloud, fog and thunder-storms. Actual flying, however, especially by night, is the most important part of the curriculum. The bombing pilot must learn, above all, to keep formation, for on his ability to do so the safety of a whole squadron may depend. The highest standard of proficiency is demanded before the young airman is allowed to take part in an actual raid.

The training of pilots has been facilitated by the extended use of the Link Trainer, to which reference has already been made. This is a mechanical device for reproducing on the ground the motions of an aeroplane in flight. It consists of a dummy fuselage and a cockpit mounted on a pedestal and so balanced that the movement of the controls produces positions similar to those which manipulation in the air would produce. In the past the Link Trainer has been used only for instruction in " blind " flying, the pilot's head being covered by a hood so that he has to rely entirely upon the instruments on the dashboard. It has recently been adapted to visual flying instruction, the fuselage being set up in a large circular room, on the walls of which are representations of sky, landscape, towns, countryside, etc. The fuselage is driven by powerful bellows and steered on its turntable through all the motions of flight. The pupil, using the controls, takes off, turns, banks, rises, descends and so on. If he goes off his course, puts his nose too much down or applies too much bank, the instructor can correct him at once. Flying instruction of a simple character can thus be given indoors, and the period of elementary instruction reduced (it is estimated) by one-fifth.

The Men on the Ground

The training of the ground staff of the Royal Air Force is no less comprehensive and complete than that of the flying *personnel*. The tradesmen, in particular, are put through a course of instruction which is probably more exacting than that required in any other air service. In the Royal Air Force a distinction is drawn, for the purpose of recruitment and training, between the mechanics whose responsibility is highest and those who work, for the most part, under supervision. The former are classed in " Group I " ; they are the fitters, the instrument makers, the machine tool setters and operators, the metal workers, and the wireless and electrical mechanics. The fitters are subdivided into fitters (airframe), fitters (engine), fitters (armourer) and fitters (torpedo). " Group II " includes armourers, balloon operators, carpenters, electricians, flight mechanics, flight riggers, instrument repairers, photographers, and wireless operators. Other Groups include fabric workers, equipment assistants (in effect, storemen), teleprinter operators, drivers (petrol), aircraft hands —the " privates " of the Air Force—and such callings as those of the cook, the butcher, the clerk and the musician.

The tradesmen of Group I are the élite of the mechanics and are trained *ab initio* by the Air Force itself. They are caught young. They come in as " aircraft apprentices," at about the age of sixteen, and go through a three years' course of instruction before being posted to squadrons or depots. The men of Group II, on the other hand, are mainly recruited at the age of eighteen or more, though some " boy entrants " are also taken in in this Group. These men of Group II have usually had some experience in civil life of the kind of work for which they are attested in the Air Force. They are given courses of instruction in the special duties which they will be called upon to perform in the service. They are not expected to attain as high a standard of skill in their trades as the men of Group I, but it is always possible for the exceptional man to rise into the higher category if he sets his heart upon it. An armourer (Group II) may, for instance, become a fitter-armourer (Group I) by attending what is called a " conversion course," for the purpose of making himself fitted for the more responsible work, and thereafter passing a trade test.

The apprentices are given theoretical as well as practical instruction ; they are taught mathematics, engineering, drawing, the principles of mechanics, and aerodynamics. The effect of airflow and its relation to the slots on a wing are studied. The internal combustion engine and its working are explained to them in detail. They are taught how to overhaul an aircraft or an engine, how to repair any breakage or defect, how to set magnetos or carburetters. The mysteries of " lift " and " drag " are made clear to them by the use of wind tunnels and whirling arms. There is little about the maintenance of an airframe or engine which the aircraft apprentice does not know by the time he has finished his course. For the really keen and intelligent boy the prospect of advancement is high in the extreme. A number of apprentices are selected for admission to the Cadet College each year, and the highest rank in the Air Force may be attained by a lad who is fortunate enough to be given such a chance to prove his worth. Even if he does not pass to the flying branch of the service, the young tradesman who has ambition and ability is assured of a satisfactory career on the technical side of the Air Force.

The importance of the technical side was emphasised when, in 1939, a separate branch of the Royal Air Force was formed for engineering, armament and signals duties. With modern equipment, the official announcement states, it is not desirable or practicable to have a body of officers to discharge both the duties of first-rate pilots and those of highly skilled technicians. Some of the posts in the new branch would be filled, it was stated, by commissioned warrant officers of the Royal Air Force. Other *personnel* for it would be found from university graduates, preferably those who had taken engineering or natural science degrees ; from engineering students who had had some years' experience in large civil works and had continued their technical education to the standard of a second class honours degree ; and from engineers who had acquired theoretical knowledge up to a University degree standard and had also had practical experience of engineering work. The inauguration of a technical branch was a recognition of the highly specialised character of the duties of the technical officers of the Air Force.

TWENTY TO ONE

It has been computed that at least twenty men are needed on the ground for each man who goes into the air. The pilots, observers, gunners and wireless operators are necessarily only a small proportion of the total strength of an air force. That does not mean that all the men on the ground are engaged in maintenance of the aircraft or engines or in other technical duties. The duties of the ground staff are multiform. It does mean, however, that if air power is to be organised on a great scale, the strength of the air arm of the State concerned must be in war of a magnitude comparable to that of its whole peace-time army ; indeed, for a country like Great Britain, of greater magnitude. Already the Royal Air Force is considerably larger than the regular army was a few years ago.

In 1934 the maximum strength of the Royal Air Force, as fixed by Vote A in the Air Estimates, was 32,000 officers and men. In the Air Estimates for 1939–40, Vote A provided for a maximum of 118,000, and the supplementary Estimates presented in July, 1939, increased that figure to 150,000. The growth of the Auxiliary Air Force was still more striking. In 1934 the *personnel* numbered 15,000 ; in 1939 it had become 104,000. Sir Kingsley Wood, in his speech on the Air Estimates on 9th March, 1939, was able to inform the House of Commons that in less than nine months the number of pilots, observers, airmen and boys taken into the regular Air Force was greater than that of the whole Air Force of a year or two earlier. A year later, on 7th March, 1940, he told the House that the strength of one Air Force Command alone had nearly reached the figure of 100,000. What the total strength of the Force was he did not disclose. It is probably not very far below that reached at the end of the last war, that is, after four years of fighting. It was then nearly 300,000; and there were about 25,000 cadets under flying instruction. It is evident that, as this war progresses, we shall see in being in this country a vast army of the air far surpassing anything that would have seemed even remotely possible in the piping times of peace of pre-expansion Britain.

Such a growth will be materially assisted by the change in higher administration announced on 2nd July, 1940, when the appointment of a new member of the Air Council was made known. The Air Member for Training, as he is termed, is responsible for training policy and the success of the training programme, and also for ensuring that the training organisation is at all times adequate to meet the needs of the Service. The object, it was stated, was to speed up the training of pilots, air crews and ground *personnel* to keep pace with the increased production of aircraft. The appointment under him of three Directors of Training—Operational, Flying and Technical—was announced on 30th July.

CHAPTER 6

BOMBERS AT WORK

THE ACID TEST

THE claim made in the two preceding chapters that the machines and the men of the Royal Air Force are preeminent in quality could hardly be sustainable if what had happened in this present war to date had shown them to be distinctly mediocre. War is the acid test. It is the final examination to which the airman must submit after his long course of training, the last trial which the aircraft must undergo if it is to confirm its showing in the exercises of peace. How, in fact, have our pilots, air crews and aircraft fared in this war up to the present ? What have they actually done ? Are their achievements such as support the view that they are about as good as men and machines can be ? Is it mere self-deception to claim that they have no cause to fear comparison with the *personnel* and *matériel* of any other country ?

In answer to that question the writer tries to illustrate in the present and following chapters the work of the bombing, fighter and other units of the Royal Air Force in the war now in progress. It is the most practical, indeed, the only practical answer to the question. It is in any case relevant to another question which must arise in a book dealing with air power. Air power, by itself, is more or less an abstraction. It means little or much according to one's initial conception of the scope of the term. It means something quite definite and concrete when analysed and split up into power to bomb, to fight, to reconnoitre in the air. Only by thinking of what our air squadrons of the various kinds actually do, and making allowance for future developments, such as the increase in strength that we may confidently look forward to and the adoption of a more vigorous policy in the air, can we obtain a true picture of what British air power means.

The Bombing Command is one of the four operational Commands of the Royal Air Force. The others are the Fighter, Coastal and Balloon Commands. The last is hardly in line with the other three. Its role is more comparable to that of the anti-aircraft and searchlight organisations which are part of the Army, not of the Royal Air Force. It comes into contact with the enemy only in the same circumstances ; its units do not go out and engage the enemy before the defended points are reached ; they are, in short, more passive—which is not to say that their work is not of great importance. The Balloon Command, it may be added, was established only in 1939, as were also the Maintenance and Reserve Commands, whose duties are, respectively, to administer all storage units and depots of the Royal Air Force at home, and to train all sections of the Volunteer Reserve, including pilots, air crews and ground *personnel*.

The Bombing Command has at its head an Air Officer Commanding-in-Chief. It administers a number of Groups, each in charge of an Air Vice-Marshal, and these in turn control the stations and squadrons in which the bombing force is distributed. The bombing force is essentially the offensive force of the air arm. Its role is defensive only in so far as, by bombing, it reduces or limits the volume of attack which the enemy can bring to bear upon this country. It is not defensive in the same direct way as the Fighter Command is defensive. Bombers do not ordinarily fight bombers. Their primary function is to bomb ; secondary functions, namely to reconnoitre and to assist in propaganda, must now be recognised as being assigned to them also, but bombing remains their most important task.

In Poland and again in Finland the bombers have had ample scope to exploit their capabilities. In both, when employed against military objectives—aerodromes, troop concentrations, railway junctions, lines of communications—they have had an undoubted effect upon the issue of many tactical operations. " It has been proved decisively," said " a Military Correspondent " in *The Times* of 11th September, 1939, referring to the operations in Poland, " that a great superiority in the air is an advantage to an attacking army which it is impossible to over-estimate." It was by low-flying attacks, the Correspondent added, that the German aircraft were able to intervene most effectively. Dive-bombing was resorted to in the Polish campaign on a great scale. The experience gained in the Spanish civil war was particularly useful in the new theatre. In Spain the Junkers Ju 87, a two-seater single-engined bomber, had been used very successfully in dive-bombing attacks on many occasions—in the operations on the Ebro, for instance, and in the Catalonian offensive, as well as against the ports of Valencia, Tarragona and Barcelona. In Poland the same machine and also the Henschel Hs 123 were extensively employed for dive-bombing attacks, mostly at very low altitudes. In Finland, on the other hand, the bombing was mainly conducted from heights of 10,000 feet or more. In Norway, too, the German dive-bombers had a decisive effect upon the operations around Trondheim. It was their destruction of the landing facilities at Aandalsnes and Namsos which led to the withdrawal of the Allies' forces from that region.

DIVE-BOMBING AND "PRECISION"

Dive-bombing is generally considered to be more accurate than high-level or (so-called) "precision" bombing. The latter kind of attack may be conducted from any height within the aircraft's ceiling, and this may be as much as six miles high, though normally the height is very much less. A level approach has to be made by the bomber in this kind of attack, and the anti-aircraft guns, with their predictors, are then given their chance to score a hit. The bomb has to be released some miles before the aircraft is vertically above its target. If something in Hyde Park were the objective, for instance, an aircraft coming from the north at a height of, say, 20,000 feet would have to loose its bomb when over Hampstead Heath. The bomb would strike at about the same time as the aircraft was vertically above the target.

An alternative to "precision" bombing is "pattern" bombing, that is, the peppering of an area with a large number of bombs in the expectation that some of them will hit the objective, assumed to be in the centre.

This kind of bombing is also carried out at considerable altitude and in this respect differs from low-level and dive-bombing. In low-level bombing the aircraft relies upon the element of surprise and advantage has to be taken of suitable weather conditions if this mode of attack is to be adopted. In dive-bombing the approach is made at considerable heights and the bomb is released at anything from 2,000 feet to 200 feet vertically from the target. Only machines which are strong enough to sustain the stresses set up in the dive and the pull-out can be employed in this form of attack ; they usually have some kind of air brake to control the speed of the dive.

During the first eight months of the war the rôle of our bombers had been reconnaissance rather than bombing. Only a few bombs were dropped on land, and these, one may surmise, were intended for objectives on the water nearby (as at Bridge of Wraith) or were dropped in retaliation (as in our attack on Sylt three days later, 19th March, 1940). The reconnaissance were conducted to a large extent by night and the black-out of the districts flown over has made it difficult to identify particular localities. (How effective the black-out can be is shown by the fact that one of our own Coastal Command aircraft, after an encounter with a Dornier in the North Sea, flew with a damaged rudder right across England and nearly to the Isle of Man before its pilot found that he had overshot the mark and turned back—to land safely.) The difficulty of observation by night is overcome in some degree by the use of parachute flares. The flare is carried in a tubular case and has a small parachute attached to it, as well as a vane which causes an explosion when the case has fallen a certain distance. The explosion ignites the flare and blows both flare and parachute out of the tubular case. The parachute opens and floats downwards with the flare, which burns with a brilliant light for nearly ten minutes, illuminating the ground below.

Reconnaissance has been combined with the dropping of leaflets for the purpose of propaganda. Millions of such leaflets were scattered over Germany, Austria, Czecho-Slovakia and Poland, while German aircraft have dropped leaflets here and in France. The bombers used by us for this purpose were mainly Whitley V's[1] and most of the leaflet raids started from England.

THE WHITLEY REJUVENATED

The Armstrong-Whitworth Whitley is a curious example of rejuvenation. This machine was exhibited among the experimental types and without a name at the Royal Air Force Display at Hendon in 1935. Next year, 1936, it appeared under the name Whitley and was described as a " heavy bomber "; in 1935 it had been designated a " bomber transport landplane." It was becoming a veteran in 1939, and with its rather poor speed was hardly in the same class as the more modern machines. Then, however, a kind of surgical operation was performed upon it. It was given two Rolls-Royce Merlin engines of 1,030 horse-power each, instead of its former Armstrong-Siddeley Tiger engines of 918 horse-power. The result was similar to that claimed for the treatment of human beings with monkey

[1] Wellingtons and Hampdens were also used on long-range reconnaissance flights by night, and Blenheims by day, and all four types have carried out many bombing operations since the spring.

glands. The machine was given a new lease of life, renewed vigour and greatly augmented usefulness. Its appearance, however, was not much improved. It was, and still is, about the most sinister thing in the air ; a very long deep-fuselaged body with a trap-door at the nose, the embodiment of volatilised evil. Other bombers look as if they might have a little good, at least, about them. The Whitley looks wicked all through.

The Whitley V bombers[1] have a number of notable flights to their credit in the present war. One of the most remarkable was that of 7th–8th March, 1940, when they started in daylight from England and returned next morning to a base in France, having been in the air for ten hours and covered a total distance of 1,500 miles. The flight of the night of 12th–13th January was another fine achievement. It started from and returned to France ; the bombers split up into two groups, one making for a more northerly and the other a southern destination. Some of the aircraft engaged in this flight covered 1,000 miles and were in the air for over nine hours. These flights were completely thrown into the shade by one carried out in a Wellington from Scotland to Narvik and along the Norwegian coast at the end of April. It lasted over fourteen hours and covered more than 2,000 miles. On none of these flights were the bombers attacked either in the air or from the ground. Indeed, the absence of any opposition has been a remarkable feature of many of the long-distance reconnaissances.

In the five long night-flights which our Whitleys carried out at the end of February and the beginning

[1] The Whitley V has a later mark of Merlin engine than the Whitley IV.

95

of March, and which in some instances involved ten hours' flying, anti-aircraft guns came into action against the bombers only on two occasions—on the nights of 1st and 2nd March. They had done so also on the occasion of the first flight of this duration, that on 26th October, when the pilot of one of the bombers dived down to reach a warmer atmosphere and, it was reported, " the defence fired every gun it could bring to bear." At another large town the pilot came down to 4,000 feet to make a closer inspection, and found himself in the centre of what he described as " bucket-fuls " of projectiles. To avoid them he went headlong down 3,000 feet farther, and so upset the gunners' aim that he escaped untouched.[1] On other occasions the raiders have been pelted with " flaming onions," which are strings of balls of fire shot up in the path of the aircraft with the object of setting it ablaze. Special incendiary shells which discharge large red balls of fire have also been encountered by our bombers. One of our machines returned from a flight on 27th November with only the framework of one of its wings left and with half the other missing.

SECURITY PATROL

Another of the routine duties of our Bomber Command for many months was the carrying out of " security patrols " in the Heligoland Bight. In these patrols one can see the application to a new problem of a solution which had been found for one arising in very different circumstances elsewhere. A practice which had already been adopted with successful results

[1] *The Times*, 13th November, 1939.

WHITLEY BOMBER

This machine is just returning from a long distance reconnaissance flight over German territory. It brings information which will set bombers speeding to their targets.

Official Photograph)

THE STING IN THE TAIL

The formidable rear gun turret of a Whitley. The armament of British bombers has made them more than a match for German fighters.

(Official Photograph)

The rear gun turret of a Whitley Bomber as a German pilot may see it at his risk.

Official Photograph)

by our Royal Air Force on the North-west Frontier of India was transferred to a Western setting. There, rebellious tribesmen are kept in check by the simple device of an air patrol which flies regularly over their villages when the signs of incipient revolt are detected. Very occasionally it may be necessary to drop a bomb or two, but this is never done until a warning has been given that the place is to be bombed and should be vacated. Ordinarily, the mere presence of a few bombers, or a single bomber, flying round and round the sky over the disaffected district, is enough to induce the villagers to amend their ways.

So, in December, 1939, a " security patrol " was instituted over Sylt, Norderney and Borkum for the purpose of preventing the seaplanes whose bases are in these waters from leaving in the evening to lay magnetic or other mines on the English coast. The effect was to pin the seaplanes to their moorings, just as the Mahsuds were pinned to their caves by our circumnavigating aircraft, and thus to prevent them from getting up to mischief. Seaplanes cannot safely take off or land unless a flare path is laid out on the water, and it was the task of the security patrol to see that no such path was laid. They were there to say, in effect, " Put out those lights ! " The story that they took an A.R.P. warden with them to certify that the black-out was effective was not, however, corroborated authoritatively. The black-out was enforced by the mere presence of the bombers. It was usually sufficient for them to approach the moorings to have all the lights promptly switched off. Only occasionally was it necessary to drop bombs to force the flare path to be extinguished.

The security patrols thus became a routine duty of the Bomber Command, but not one that was free from its excitements or, it may be added, its perils. Each patrol involved a flight of five or six hours' duration, over 800 miles of sea. Near the islands the bombers might be met, at height, with fire from anti-aircraft guns of large calibre. If they ventured lower, fire from pom-poms and machine-guns on hangar roofs at the seaplane stations might be encountered. If enemy fighters did not attack, they hung about the sky to warn the ground batteries of the approach of the patrolling bombers. The weather might be atrocious. There was always the danger of fog—the North Sea is a breeding-ground for fogs. There was the possibility of ice forming on the controls even at 500 feet over the sea. Then there was the strain of night flying, relieved only partly by reliance on the automatic pilot, the " George " of the Royal Air Force. The life of the airmen who made these nightly visits to the Heligoland Bight was assuredly not lacking in interest.

Our bombers, it should be added, themselves took a hand in mine-laying after the German invasion of Norway on 9th April. It was disclosed on 6th July that during the preceding three months they had laid great numbers of mines along the whole coastline of Germany and also of Norway, with highly successful results. In two of the minefields alone at least twelve ships had been sunk, and in another five had shared the same fate in a space of thirty-six hours.

Air power in its more positive and active manifestation is bombing power. If the air arm is to be a decisive factor in war it must rely on the bomber to achieve that result. In comparison the function of the fighter is preventive or ancillary. It is preventive in so far as it can immobilise the bomber. It is ancillary in so far as it can protect the bomber from being intercepted or interfered with by enemy fighters. It may be that the fighter alone can win supremacy in the air. The task of exploiting that supremacy, when won, falls on the bomber.

THE BOMBERS GET BUSY

It was only in April, 1940, that our bombers were given their first opportunity to attack land targets. The German invasion of Norway was very largely an invasion by air-carried contingents, and the aerodromes used for this purpose were therefore an obvious target. Between 10th April and 3rd May, 1940, the aerodrome at Stavanger was bombed almost nightly and sometimes by day as well. Those at Fornebo and Kjeller, near Oslo, at Trondheim, at Aalborg and Ry in Denmark, and at Westerland in Sylt were also attacked. Much damage was done to the runways and hangars and a considerable number of German aircraft were destroyed or severely damaged. Oil tanks at Valle in Oslo Fjord and at other places were attacked at the same time and also by aircraft of the Fleet Air Arm in May.

On 10th May a new era began. The German invasion of Holland and Belgium was accompanied by air attacks on road and rail communications in these countries and also on aerodromes in France. Our bombers eagerly seized their new opportunity. " After eight months of patient waiting," wrote a war correspondent a few days later, " the bomber squadrons of the

Advanced Air Striking Force have had their first real chance of aiming a blow at the enemy this week-end (11th to 13th May), and they have taken the fullest advantage of it. Raid after raid has been successfully carried out on the German troops moving forward through Luxemburg and Belgium, and many of our pilots have come back with heartening stories showing clearly the havoc they have caused."[1]

The correspondent goes on to tell how Blenheims and Battles attacked heavy concentrations of German troops and mechanised transports behind the German lines, piled up lorries on the roads, and blocked the route with wrecked and burning vehicles. "One heavy bomb scored a direct hit in the middle of a line of forty or fifty heavy lorries." The good work went on during the subsequent days. "One of our bomber squadrons," said a later report, "attacked a bridge which the Germans had just finished building over a river near the Belgian frontier in the Ardennes district. The bridgehead house was demolished by a direct hit and the bridge itself was smashed to matchwood."[2] Roads and railways continued to be the target of our bombers, and the bigger types, Whitleys and Hampdens, were employed as well as medium bombers.

The greatest bombing attack yet seen in the war occurred on 15th May, when 150 Allied aircraft launched a combined attack on the crossings of the Meuse and the main lines of the advancing reinforcements. Four bridges were destroyed—two pontoon bridges had been destroyed in a preliminary attack—large tank and troop concentrations broken and roads blocked. " The effect

[1] *The Times*, 13th May, 1940.
[2] *The Times*, 14th May, 1940.

SHARP SHOOTERS OF THE AIR
The men who man the gun-turrets of the bombers.
(Official Photograph)

GROUND DEFENCES
R.A.F. gunners ready to defend their aerodrome against low flying attackers.
(Photo: Sport & General Press Agency Ltd.

TARGET PRACTICE
R.A.F. fighters engaged in target practice—this photograph gives some idea of what a German bomber sees when attacked by a flight of Hurricanes.

THE NEW FLEET "SPOTTER"
The Fairey Albacore, Britain's latest Fleet spotter reconnaissance bi-plane, now in service with the Fleet Air Arm. Details of performance are still secret.

of the operations," said the Air Ministry *communiqué*, " was to halt the German advance in the Sedan sector and enable the French to launch a vigorous counter-attack."

The heaviest attack yet made by the Royal Air Force itself was delivered on the night of the 16th May, against the enemy's road and rail communications to the *east* of the Rhine. The bombers were Whitleys, Wellingtons and Hampdens, and they started both from France and England. " Each crew," said the *communiqué*, " was given specific military objectives and instructions that bombs were not to be dropped indiscriminately. A few failed to locate their objectives and did not drop their bombs, but the majority found and bombed their targets with great effect, causing widespread damage and many explosions and fires." Roads, including an important *Autobahn*, railway lines and a military encampment were among the objectives ; so were mechanised columns. One direct hit resulted in an explosion of such force that the blast rocked the aircraft some thousands of feet above. A Wellington had a narrow escape when it found itself in the centre of a balloon barrage ; by banking steeply it managed to avoid the cables. A few nights later a successful raid was undertaken against petrol storage tanks at Bremen and Hamburg. Meanwhile, the usual bombing of enemy forces and their communications continued. The bombers had no reason to complain of lack of employment from the time when the great German offensive started. They had hardly time to bomb-up between raids.

Western Germany had good reason to be aware of the existence of the Bomber Command from mid-May onwards. It advertised its presence by fireworks. A fire started by our Whitley bombers on the night of 17th May could be seen at Cuxhaven, sixty miles from its actual site, and the flame from a large oil storage tank at Bremen on the same night so lit up the sky that, according to the pilot's report, " even at 10,000 feet one could have read the smallest print." A large part of western Germany was covered by " trails of blazing fires followed by explosions," stretching from Emmerich in the north to Frankfurt in the south, after our bombers had passed on the night of 3rd June. " The whole place was a mass of flames," said the captain of the last aircraft to arrive on the scene. At Mannheim, on the night of 4th June, the streaming oil from the storage tanks that had been bombed " quickly became a mass of raging flames, reddening the night sky and being visible to aircraft flying more than 100 miles away from the scene of the vast conflagration." The bombing of a power-house at Misburg, near Hanover, on the night of 18th June caused an explosion which rocked the aircraft at a height of 10,000 feet above. The blaze caused at Hamburg on the same night could be seen by our aircraft when they crossed the German coast, eighty miles away, on their homeward journey. One of the many fires which were started at Kiel on the night of 1st July was described by the last pilot to leave the scene of the bombing as " a solid mass of flame covering as much space as a big aerodrome." These were but a few of the many huge conflagrations caused by the heavy machines of the Bomber Command after deep raiding had begun in earnest. They are entirely unexplainable if our raids were directed only against villages, dwelling houses, schools, etc., as Herr Hitler alleged in his speech in the Reichstag on 19th July, 1940.

THE BRIDGE AT MAASTRICHT

This account of the work of our bombers could not end more appropriately than with the epic story of the attack by Fairey Battle bombers on the bridge at Maastricht. It is one which will be remembered " till story and song and glory and all things sleep." Here it is in the simple but intensely dramatic account given by the Air Ministry itself :

" All the bridges over the Meuse near Maastricht, where the Germans were making their thrust to divide the Allied forces, had been blown up except one. Over that bridge poured the tanks and armoured units of the enemy advance. Stores, petrol, ammunition—everything came over that one bridge. It was heavily defended. A.A. guns kept up a barrage of fire, enemy fighters maintained constant patrols.

" Eight attacks were made by our bombers. The river banks were shattered by high explosives ; fighters were shot down in flames ; A.A. batteries bombed out of action. But no direct hit was scored on the bridge. Still the enemy advances poured over that one crossing.

" At the R.A.F. squadron headquarters the Commanding Officer made a short speech to his pilots. The bridge must be destroyed. Volunteers were wanted.

" The pilots stepped forward as one man.

" So they wrote their names on slips of paper and put them in a hat. Five crews were chosen. They went off without waiting. Fighters went up as escort and they made straight for the bridge at Maastricht. Our fighters took on the enemy's fighter guard, welcoming all odds to give the bombers their chance. Facing a blizzard of enemy fire the bombers dived low on their target.

" Of those five crews one man came back.
" But the bridge at Maastricht was blown up."[1]

---

[1] Actually, there were two bridges to be destroyed, and they were over the Albert Canal, not the Meuse. The pilot, Flying Officer D. E. Garland, and the observer, Sergeant T. Gray, of the Battle which led the formation of five were awarded posthumously the Victoria Cross for their most conspicuous gallantry in this forlorn hope and, it is to be assumed, in recognition of the gallantry of the splendid young men who took part in it.

CHAPTER 7

FIGHTERS IN ACTION

CHECK TO THE BOMBERS

THE Fighter Command, it has already been stated, is one of the four operational Commands of the Royal Air Force. As organised in peace it administers two Groups, charged respectively with the air defence of the southern and the northern parts of Great Britain. It is not concerned with the defence of overseas possessions.

The relation of the fighter branch of the air arm to air power in general has already been explained briefly in Chapter 6. Its rôle is essentially defensive. It may attack ground targets, with machine-gun fire, and did so on various occasions in the last war, but that is not its normal tactical activity. Its job is to attack other aircraft, bombers, fighters or reconnaissance aircraft. Its speciality is horizontal combat. It is the destroyer of the air.

The idea that the bomber has not much to fear from the fighter prevailed for some years before the civil war in Spain came to throw doubt upon it. Many people had accepted the view of General Douhet that bombers could be made so formidable that they could fight their way through the interceptors of the enemy.

Others considered that speed was the best protection of the bomber. There was, indeed, little to choose in the matter of speed, or performance in general, between the light bombers of a few years ago, such as the British Harts, and the biplane fighters of that time, such as the Bulldogs or Furies. There was little dissent from the current dogma that " the bomber will always get through." " I think it is well for the man in the street to realise," said Mr. (now Earl) Baldwin in the House of Commons on 10th November, 1932, " that there is no power on earth which can prevent him from being bombed. Whatever people may tell him, the bomber will always get through. . . . The only defence is in offence, which means that you have to kill more women and children more quickly than the enemy if you want to save yourselves."

Events in Spain in 1936–37 served to correct the perspective. In Spain the fighter pilot began to come into his own. Even when the comparatively slow and moderately armed biplane fighters were in use in the earlier part of the war they proved themselves to be dangerous enemies to the bombers. The later fighters, the multi-gun monoplanes of high speed, were still more formidable opponents. The lesson of the war in that respect was clear. " Contact once obtained," says M. Rougeron, " and given comparable equality in equipment, the superiority of the defence is certain."[1] The advantage which fighting over one's own territory gives the defence, he adds, is " enormous." " In spite of the technical and numerical inferiority of the fighters on the Government side to the machines of German

[1] C. Rougeron, *Les Enseignements Aériens de la Guerre d'Espagne*, 1939, p. 61.

and Italian construction which were opposed to them, it was possible for the former to halt, with grave losses, the nationalist raids against the Government's rear areas."[1] The fighter began indeed to give itself airs in consequence. "The *chasse* machine," says General Duval, "considers the bombing machine incapable of defending itself."[2] "It is now definitely admitted," says Capitaine Didier Poulain, "that the bomber is practically without defence against the fighter. The supremacy of the fast single-seater, so easy to manipulate in combat, is certain."[3] Bombers in Spain could only avoid heavy casualties by protecting themselves by screens of fighters, says Herr F. A. Fischer von Poturzyn.[4] Even before the present war the doctrine that " the bomber will always get through " had been recognised in this country for the half-truth that it was.

"There was a time when the problem of dealing with the bomber was regarded by the people of this country with something akin to despair," said Lord Chatfield, Minister for Co-ordination of Defence, in the House of Lords on 15th March, 1939. "Such feelings are no longer justified, if indeed they were ever justified. Developments in recent years have undoubtedly reduced the old supremacy of the offensive over the defensive in air warfare." Almost the same words had been used by Sir Kingsley Wood in the House of Commons on 9th March. "There has been in the past," he said, " a tendency to subscribe to the

[1] C. Rougeron, *Les Enseignements Aériens de la Guerre d'Espagne* 1939, p. 61.
[2] *Les Leçons de la Guerre d'Espagne*, 1938, p. 154.
[3] *Journal of the Royal United Service Institution*, August, 1938, p. 582.
[4] *Luftmacht*, 1938, p. 85.

argument that the bomber will always get through, but developments in recent years have in fact reduced the supremacy of the offensive and have added to the strength of the defensive in the air."

The view expressed by the Ministers in these statements finds support in the events of the present war. Where it has been possible to establish contact the fighters have proved their superiority to the bombers. The latter have suffered heavily in many encounters. In our own raid into the Heligoland Bight on 18th December, 1939, which was carried out by Wellington's, we had seven bombers brought down and others badly crippled. We claimed that twelve fighters were shot down on the other side, but the fact remained that our bombers were severely punished. Before that, our bombers had suffered severely in a raid over the same waters on 29th September and we also had losses in another raid on 14th December. The losses of German bombers in their raids into British territorial waters were no less striking. Over sixty had been brought down by our fighters before the more intensive raiding of this country began in June, 1940, and others, there was good reason to believe, failed to reach home after their clashes with our defence. Their number has been very greatly increased since 18th June. The evidence to support the proposition that the bomber will *not* always get through is, so far, conclusive.

How will it be affected by future developments? The bombers will become better fitted to protect themselves, one may surmise. They will profit from the experience gained as the war progresses. They will have armoured protection for their crews, fire-

DEFIANTS ON
THE WING

The Boulton-Paul
Defiant Fighter is a
two seater monoplane
with a Rolls-Royce
Merlin engine and a
multiple gun turret
amidships. It is the
fastest plane of its
class in service and
the only land fighter
in the world with a
revolving turret.

(*Official Photograph*)

THE DEFIANT'S TURRET
It was this turret which enabled the Defiant to do such terrible execution above Dunkirk.
(Photo: Barratt's Photo Press Ltd., London)

WAITING FOR THE WORD
A Boulton-Paul Defiant fighter ready to take off. It will be seen that like all the latest type of high-speed aircraft this machine has a triple-bladed screw and retractable undercarriage.
(Official Photograph)

proof petrol tanks, better armament. Will the improved performance and more powerful armament of the fighters enable the latter to maintain their predominance? That is a question which only time can answer. It is a very important question in its bearing upon the wider question of the influence of British air power upon the issue of the war.

THE FIGHTER COMMAND

There are three ways in which the fighter component of the air arm can contribute to that influence. The first is by safeguarding the homeland from invasion by air. This island of Great Britain is the heart of the Empire. Its survival is a condition precedent to the successful emergence of the British Commonwealth of Nations from the ordeal by battle to which it has been committed. Britain itself must stand or the war cannot be won. As Liddell Hart has rightly insisted, the security of the " home base " is the first and most essential item in any strategic programme.[1]

At the beginning of this war it was commonly thought that the chief task of the Fighter Command would be the protection of our populated centres from enemy air attack. The expected raids did not come, and the Command had for many months to devote itself to a different kind of employment. It has had to meet the tip-and-run raids upon Scapa Flow and Rosyth by small numbers of German aircraft and to intercept single reconnaissance machines which rarely venture beyond high-water mark on our coasts. It has had

[1] Liddell Hart, *The Defence of Britain*, 1939, p. 159.

to defend merchant vessels and fishing boats, perhaps far out at sea, against bombing and machine-gunning. It has also had to drive off enemy seaplanes which try to lay mines along our coasts. All these duties have meant a great increase in the activities of the Command. During the first month of the war the mileage flown was only 200,000. In the Spring of 1940 it had risen to about 2,000,000 a month. The fighters have to patrol a 700-mile coastline up to a height of five miles.

It is on the fighter squadrons which we must rely in the first place for the defence of this island from air attack on an unprecedented scale. The ground defence is important, too, but it is defence in the air which will break the onslaught. Will it do so ? The great test has yet to come, but the omens are propitious and the grounds for a sober confidence substantial. " Successful defence depends on what happens to the enemy when he is intercepted," said Sir Hugh Dowding, the chief of the Fighter Command, in an interview shortly before the present war began. " I can confidently say that I am satisfied in this respect." The achievements of his men and his machines since he spoke have justified his confidence. Where they can make contact they can break the attack. There is no reason why they should not be as successful when the attack is of far greater magnitude, for the defence then will have been augmented, too, and its equipment improved. The output of Spitfires and Hurricanes doubled itself in the six months after Sir Hugh Dowding spoke, and it may safely be assumed that a still greater increase has since taken place ; the speed of the Spitfires has been increased, as compared with the earlier model, by 10 per cent.[1] Neither the Spitfire nor the Hurricane is the final entry, moreover, in the stud-book of our bloodstock of the air.

The only doubt is whether it will always be possible to make contact. The sky is large. The raider has a lot of room in which to come and go. He may have to be met at any level from zero to thirty thousand feet or more. The Heinkel bomber which was shot down off the Aberdeen coast on 7th March, 1940, was engaged by our Spitfires at a height of more than five miles above sea-level. The Heinkel, one of its engines out of action, glided down from that great height towards the land, with the Spitfires in pursuit, and finally alighted on the sea. A few weeks earlier, on 13th February, three Spitfires had dived fourteen thousand feet to try to intercept another Heinkel off the mouth of the Thames ; it eluded them by taking cover in a cloud, but they delivered some bursts of fire as they dived. Compare these combats with the pursuit of another Heinkel by Squadron-Leader A. D. Farquhar's fighters over the roof-tops of Edinburgh on 16th October, 1940. Interception in an element of three dimensions is never exactly automatic, and when there are clouds to afford cover it is a game of baffling hide-and-seek. All that one can say is that, as the raids on Britain since 18th June have shown, in a fair proportion of cases it should be possible for the fighters, aided by wireless direction, to make contact, and that in a substantial percentage of the cases in which contact is made a kill should follow. Between the beginning of the war and 31st August, 1940, 1,419 enemy aircraft

[1] Statement of Sir Kingsley Wood in the House of Commons, 7th March, 1940.

had been brought down over and off our coasts, and our total loss in these defensive operations was 351 fighters.

DEFENDING BRITAIN'S COASTS

Indeed, in one category of defensive operations the events of the war have shown that it is possible for fighters to make contact with enemy raiders more frequently than some experts had predicted. It had been supposed that the protection of ports and shipping therein, or in territorial waters, from air attack would be a matter of great difficulty. Even if the raiders do not adopt the method of " silent approach " which was practised against Barcelona and other ports of Spain, and the technique of which consists in the cutting-off of the engine or engines at a great height and then gliding down towards the objective,[1] they are still able to launch their bombs without coming nearer to the land than a distance of three miles or even more. At sea, M. Rougeron points out, it is impracticable to organise the same network of warning which is possible on land.[2] A raid against a seaside town can materialise in a few minutes, perhaps a few seconds, before the bomber is in reach of its objective. The warning is too belated to allow the fighter aircraft or the artillery to come into action. An aircraft flying at a speed of 300 kilometres (a low speed to-day), at a height of 4,000 metres, must approach to within 2,300 metres before it launches its bombs. If the speed is 500 kilo-

[1] See J. Langdon-Davies, *Air Raid*, 1938. The first gliding attack of this kind against a British objective occurred on 8th July, 1940. (*The Times*, 9th July, 1940.)
[2] C. Rougeron, *Les Enseignements Aériens de la Guerre d'Espagne*, 1939, p. 62.

metres and the altitude is 6,500 metres it need not come nearer than 5,000 metres. Even if warning is given, it still has time, after loosing its bombs, to swing away and to escape before there is much danger of its being hit. " Against coastal objectives," says M. Rougeron, " bombing operations are almost as free of risk as simple operations of transport."[1]

Both our own and the German bombers have learnt, to their cost, that the raiding of the enemy's territorial waters is very far from being the " simple operation of transport " which M. Rougeron predicted. In our raid into the Heligoland Bight on 29th September, five out of six bombers were brought down by the German fighters, according to the German official report; our own official *communiqué* merely stated that some " of our aircraft have not yet returned." In the subsequent raids on 14th and 18th December, as already stated, we also had severe losses. So did the German bombers on numerous occasions when they ventured into too close proximity to our coast. Even when a convoy was attacked, on 21st October, 1939, our fighters were able to engage the enemy aircraft well over the North Sea and to bring down four of them.[2] It is evident that fighters can come into action very much more promptly and effectively in the circumstances envisaged by M. Rougeron than he had foreseen.

Our Hurricanes and Spitfires were able to shoot down 15 of the 80 German aircraft which raided Dover

[1] C. Rougeron, *Les Enseignements Aériens de la Guerre d'Espagne*, 1939, p. 62.
[2] Three others failed to reach home. The German machines were twin-engined Heinkel He.115 seaplanes, according to *The Aeroplane*, 2nd November, 1939.

H

Harbour in the early hours of 29th July, 1940, two more being brought down by anti-aircraft fire, and to prevent a single bomb from being dropped on shore ; all in a space of 30 minutes.

ST. GEORGE'S DRAGONS

The second way in which the fighters contribute their quota of effort to that dynamic condition which constitutes the exercise of air power is by establishing supremacy in the air, for the air force of which they form part. Here it is an affair not of fighters *versus* bombers but of fighters *versus* fighters. The battle is one of hawks, of kestrels, of jerfalcon against peregrine, not of the bird of prey which swoops on its unequal victim and strikes it mercilessly down. The odds are, or should be, more even here. Here, in the highest degree, is the battle of the clouds seen in its glory, recalling the contests of jousting knights at Camelot or Carcasonne ; but how it would have amazed those antique warriors ! It is rather, indeed, a vision of St. George and the dragon that one should call up, only St. George has somehow got inside the dragon and the dragon is a flying one. St. George, that admirable Cappadocian, would have thought the seven wonders of the world had all been rolled into one and then magnified a thousandfold if he had foreseen it all.

They are, when one comes to think of it, in the modern fighter aircraft. The pilot has every imaginable scientific device at his finger ends. He can communicate, through empty space, with his commander on the ground or in the air. By pulling back a lever he can climb—on nothing—to a height of 20,000 feet in less than ten minutes. By pushing it forward he can go hurtling down at a speed approaching that of sound. By touching a button he can set a whole battery of machine-guns spitting lead at the rate of 160 rounds a second. That is the dragon, breathing fire. It is all black magic, satanic wizardry, unimaginable mystery. Even in this age of marvels there is probably no marvel to compare with the fighter aircraft.

Think of the " gadgets " it has. Take the cine-camera, for instance. This is connected with the eight machine-guns and comes into action automatically when the pilot presses the trigger-button which fires the guns. When the guns cease firing the camera ceases to take " shots." With each new burst of fire it begins to take pictures again. They are not taken for amusement or as a historical record of the fight in the air. Their purpose is much more practical. They are developed and shown on the screen in a darkened room, and from a scrutiny of the film the pilot can see what happened in those few seconds of sound and fury, what mistakes he made, what hits he recorded, how near he was to scoring a bull's-eye in some bursts of fire, how far in others. The film is run through again and again ; it can be stopped at any point so that exactly what happened just then can be made clear. The enemy's fire can be seen on the film, too, in the form of streaks across it showing the direction which the bullets took. The whole film is an object-lesson for the budding pilot ; he can learn from it the secrets of success or failure in the battle of the clouds.

Before the war it was often predicted that the day

of the old " dog-fight " in the air was over. It was thought that the immense speeds at which fighter machines engage to-day would rule out the kind of rough-and-tumble mêlée which was common in the last war. Running fights between formations of fighters, flying wing to wing, were thought to be more likely to be the rule. Actually, the dog-fight is by no means a thing of the past. It has reappeared more than once in the encounters of the present war. Manœuvreability has been proved to be as important an asset as speed in these engagements. It has been because it excels in this respect that the French Curtiss Hawk was able to hold its own with the German fighters, though the latter had an advantage in speed of fifty miles or more an hour.

The third way in which the Fighter Command aligns itself in the array of British air power is in affording protection to the striking force both in the zone of battle and in those bombing missions which are within the fighters' radius of action. Here, again, the battle in the clouds is joined, for the hostile interceptors may be encountered, and this, too, is really a part of the struggle for supremacy in the air. Our fighter pilots have no reason to fear the result of the conflict. Man for man, they have shown themselves to be better than the enemy's best. Already many of our fighter pilots would be " aces," if such a distinction were recognised in the Air Force. They have ten or more crashes of enemy machines to their credit ; and in the British service only the authenticated " kill " counts. They have proved that the British fighter is master of the prima facie more formidable Messerschmitt Me 110. " In the air," said Mr. Churchill, in his first

WRECKAGE
OF A MESSER-
SCHMITT

Officers examin-
ing the wreckage
of a German
Messerschmitt
too shot down
after it had
crossed the South
East Coast.

**BLACKBURN
SKUAS**

These powerful low-wing monoplanes are in service in the Fleet Air Arm.

(Photo:
*Charles E. Brown
London*)

broadcast as Prime Minister on 19th May, 1940, " even at serious odds, even at odds hitherto thought overwhelming, we have been clawing down three or four to one of our enemies, and the relative balance of British and German air forces is now considerably more favourable to us than at the beginning of the war." Germany's losses in France and Belgium in May amounted to at least two thousand aircraft, probably a fifth of her first-line strength. The odds referred to by Mr. Churchill were at times fantastic. An Air Ministry announcement of 14th May stated :

" In one encounter three Hurricanes attacked thirty enemy bombers and their fighter escorts near Veuzières. One Me 110 and one He 111 were shot down. In this fight a Hurricane forced another He 111 to crash, landed beside the enemy aircraft and took the crew prisoner."

The word *attacked* will be noted here. It was simply amazing impudence on the part of the three Hurricanes, but it came off ; and the Air Force is chock-full of such young desperadoes.

AN EPIC OF NORWAY

Wonderful things have been and will be done by British fighter pilots in this war, yet it is doubtful whether any achievement will be more glorious than that of the Gladiator fighter squadron which was dispatched to an improvised base in southern Norway

towards the end of April, 1940. To make an aerodrome for the squadron, the snow on the frozen lake
of Lesjeskogen, forty miles south-east of Aandalsnes,
was dug away to form a runway. An aircraft carrier
brought the Gladiators from a British port and, escorted
by aircraft of the Fleet Air Arm, they took off from
the carrier at some distance from the Norwegian coast
and flew through a blinding snowstorm to their tem-
porary base.

All the aircraft made a safe landing, and in little
over an hour were refuelled and dispersed round the
lake, except one section which was held in immediate
readiness. Though it was now late at night, it was
necessary for some of the aircraft to take off at once
to intercept two aircraft which approached. The
latter bore Norwegian markings, but were probably
flown by German pilots, and it was thus, no doubt,
that the enemy became aware of our dispositions.

At three o'clock the next morning, the Gladiators
were in the air, patrolling the area. The difficulty of
getting them into the air was immense on account of
the bitter cold. Shortly after 4 a.m., three of them
engaged a Heinkel and shot it down, and two others
were intercepted. Soon afterwards, the frozen lake
which was serving as their aerodrome was attacked by
another Heinkel with bombs and machine-gun fire.
At 7.30 a.m. the enemy began attacks which continued
without remission until eight o'clock at night.

Except on the actual runway, melting snow piled in
drifts some feet in depth made it almost impossible
to move. The British pilots were forced to crawl
through the snow on hands and knees. Their clothing
became drenched and immediately froze. All through

the ceaseless attacks to which the landing ground was subjected the pilots remained in the open ; there was no cover whatever. Exposed all the time to the enemy's bombs, they continued to come down from their combats in the air, to refuel, to replenish their ammunition and to start up their machines again. One by one their aircraft were destroyed. As they were, the pilots, some of them badly burned, helped one another to get the few remaining aircraft into the air. Meanwhile they were being incessantly machine-gunned. Those who had no machines left to fly continued to resist from the ground with a machine-gun.

Towards evening all the ammunition was exhausted, and then the pilots made attacks which were only feints, there being no means of returning the enemy's fire. One pilot, who had no ammunition and practically no petrol left and was attacked by three Messerschmitt Me 110's, saved his aircraft from being shot down by attempting again and again to ram the enemy machines until they swerved away from him. Shells from their cannons struck his aircraft repeatedly, and eventually it was set on fire. The pilot made a successful forced landing. In his own words : " I walked away and tried to start another, but was forced to leave as it was bombed and destroyed."

Another pilot had sixteen combats in all on that first day, and altogether our Gladiators engaged thirty-seven aircraft, of which they brought down six for certain and most probably eight others as well. The frozen lake which was their base was bombed and machine-gunned by eighty or ninety German bombers in all, and 132 craters could be counted upon it. By the end of the day, of the eighteen Gladiators only five were still serviceable. On the next day, these five machines carried on the hopelessly unequal combat, with the result that by the end of this second day only one aircraft remained serviceable. The squadron had " perished but prevailed."

It is a story which will live, that of the air fighting above the frozen lake near Aandalsnes. Squadron-Leader Donaldson's Gladiator squadron is but one of many whose skill and gallantry are no less high and whose equipment is more modern. Gladiators had to be sent to Norway because they can take off and land in a more restricted space than the faster monoplane fighters. The latter have proved in many a combat that they have the whiphand over the German fighters. Even against considerable odds they have shown repeatedly that the British fighter pilot and the British fighter machine are *sans pareil*.

" In one spectacular dog-fight," wrote a war correspondent in France[1], " in which twenty-seven enemy machines were tackled by a dozen British Hurricanes, the Germans were shot down so fast that a trail of blazing enemy aircraft lighted the sky from Roulers to the coast." " Our fighter pilots had a good day," said an Air Ministry *communiqué* of 16th May, 1940, referring to the fighting on 15th May. " There was no lack of targets, and attacks were pressed home from dawn to dusk. A formation of six Hurricanes attacked twenty-five Messerschmitt 110's and shot down five. In another case two Hurricanes intercepted nine Messerschmitt 110's and shot down four. Four other encounters resulted in a loss to the enemy of twenty aircraft. In all, during the day fifty enemy aircraft

[1] Douglas Williams in the *Daily Telegraph*, 14th May, 1940.

were destroyed. The *moral* of our pilots and crews could not be higher. The daily toll inflicted on enemy aircraft is working out at more than three to one in our favour."

Two Hurricane squadrons met the full fury of the German air attack on the opening day of the great offensive (10th May). They fought from before sunrise until after dusk, making one sortie after another, coming to ground only to refuel and to fill up with ammunition and then at once taking off again. Some of the pilots took off seven times. Two of them were shot down in flames; they escaped by parachute, rejoined their squadrons and at once went up again. In that one day no less than forty-nine enemy aircraft were shot down for certain, and many others probably never reached home. Our Hurricane units did not lose a single pilot. It was an extraordinary achievement, and it was not a flash in the pan. Every day for some weeks these pilots fought for five hours at least, a record for continued air fighting that is not likely to be beaten.

ENTER THE DEFIANT

It was only a little later, when the German advance reached the vicinity of the English Channel, that the home-based Spitfire squadrons came into the fight in France. Gloriously they took their part in it. A single platoon of Spitfires shot down eight Messerschmitt Me 110's on 23rd May, and probably fourteen in all, as well as three bombers. On the following day eleven Spitfires accounted for eleven Messerschmitts and seriously damaged three others; they lost not a single machine themselves. Two hours after the encounter in which they had scored this wonderful success they shot down four more Messerschmitts. Another Spitfire squadron accounted for thirteen enemy aircraft on the same day and the total " bag " for the day was forty for certain, probably more. That was indeed the average daily " bag " of our fighters in France during May. Between 10th May and 2nd June the Royal Air Force brought down, in all, 911 enemy aircraft. On one particular day, 27th May, they shot down fifty, actually seen to crash, and seriously damaged twenty-nine more. That record was surpassed two days later. On 29th May our fighters destroyed at least seventy-seven German aircraft and seriously damaged a number of others. Of the seventy-seven no less than thirty-eight were brought down by a squadron of twelve Defiants without loss to themselves. The success of this new two-seater fighter, equipped with a gun-turret, was the outstanding feature of a wonderful day. The Defiants, home-based, had only come into action when the Channel was reached by the German tide of invasion. On 12th May they drew first blood by shooting down a Junkers Ju 88 and two other enemy aircraft off the Dutch coast. On 27th May they destroyed two fighters (Me 109) and five bombers (He 111). Then on 29th May came their great day of triumph ; sixteen of their thirty-eight victims were Me 110's, the others being an Me 109 and twenty-one bombers. It was almost a battue. No single squadron had ever had such a day's hunting, nor had the total bag for the day ever been surpassed. It has since, however, been exceeded. There was a fairly heavy slaughter of German bombers and fighters, mainly over the English

Channel, in July, when in one week 85 enemy aircraft were destroyed and about 50 more seriously damaged, at a cost of 13 of our own fighters, and Mr. Churchill stated in his broadcast on 14th July that we hoped to improve on these results, as we certainly did in August, when in one day—the 15th—180 German aircraft were destroyed, the total bag for the week concerned being over 700.

CHAPTER 8

THE COASTAL COMMAND

ENDLESS VIGIL

THE Coastal Command, though it might seem at first
to be more closely related to the Navy than to the Air
Force, is an essential part of the defence by air of the
British Islands. Its units belong, of right, to the
" metropolitan air force." It is not in the same position as the naval air service—the Fleet Air Arm, as it is
still commonly called. The units of the latter and
their aircraft—the wheeled aircraft borne in the Carriers
and the seaplanes carried in the catapult ships (battleships and cruisers)—go with the Navy wherever it goes.
Their home is in all the seven seas. The hunting
ground of the Coastal Command, on the other hand, is
around these islands. Its units are shore-based.
Those of the naval air service are ship-borne.

Nevertheless, the work of the two services is similar
in so far as the task of each is largely to defend our
sea-borne commerce against naval attack, surface or
submarine. The Sunderland flying boats and the
Lockheed Hudson and Anson landplanes of the Coastal
Command spend most of their lives over blue water.
They patrol the shipping lanes, convoy merchant
vessels, hunt down submarines, locate mines, watch for

THE FLEET AIR
ARM'S
NEW FIGHTER

The Blackburn
"Roc"—a new
fighter just intro-
duced into the Fleet
Air Arm. It is
powered by a Bristol
Perseus engine and
is fitted with a
power-operated gun
turret. The perform-
ance figures are
secret.

*(Photo: Charles E.
Brown London)*

CONVOY AND PATROL
Short Sunderland flying boats guard a British convoy.

SHORT SUNDERLAND
No photograph could show more magnificently
the splendid lines of this wonderful flying boat.

the possible approach of enemy warships. But they can and do fight off enemy aircraft as well. They have had many scraps with German seaplanes and bombers in the present war.

It has been on the face of the waters and below that the airmen of the Coastal Command have mainly had to seek their prey. Submarines have been sighted in more than two hundred cases and in two-thirds of these instances bombs have been dropped. What the result of the attack has been cannot usually be known ; it may or may not have been successful. On at least one occasion, however, there has been no doubt about the result. One such instance was the destruction on 30th January, 1940, of the U-boat which had sunk the steamship *Vaclite* a little earlier. The *Vaclite* was sailing in convoy and the submarine was at once attacked by the naval escort. It was apparently damaged, for later in the same day a flying boat found it on the surface, unable to dive. A heavy bomb was dropped on the starboard side of the submarine, whose crew opened fire with their anti-aircraft gun. The flying boat replied with machine-gun fire, but the descent of cloud made further observation difficult. Warships were then directed by the flying boat to the spot where the submarine had been lying, but it had sunk by that time. A few survivors were rescued by the warships. In July a second U-boat was sunk in the south Atlantic by another Sunderland ; on this occasion, again, the survivors were rescued, a naval patrol boat being in the vicinity.

No branch of the Royal Air Force has been so continuously in action as the Coastal Command. Its units, it was reported at the end of July, had flown more than 14,000,000 miles on reconnaissance or convoy duty by that date. Not a day has passed but its squadrons have been in the air. In the foulest of weathers, in snow, gales, ice, *semi*-fog, they have kept their unending vigil. In addition to convoying merchantmen, searching for mines and harrying U-boats, they have had the task of photographing ships for the purposes of the contraband control and the policing of the seas all round these islands to guard against hostile intrusion by sea or air. They have saved scores of lives. The earliest occasion of rescue work was also the most dramatic.

On 18th September, 1939, the *Kensington Court* was torpedoed in the Atlantic. She sent out an S O S signal, which was picked up by a patrol of three flying boats. Three of the ship's boats had been launched, but one was sunk ; the remaining two were found by the flying boats, which alighted near them, and their crews, thirty-four men in all, were taken into the flying boats and flown safely to land.

The patrolling of mine-strewn waters and convoying of merchant vessels have been routine duties of the Coastal Command. Its aircraft have been the aerial sheepdogs for the flocks of ships which pass along the traffic lanes around these islands. They have saved many a vessel from destruction, sometimes only by the narrowest of margins. The Dutch steamer *Stadshiedam*, for instance, was heading for drifting mines in the North Sea when an aircraft of the Coastal Command observed the dangerous direction which she was taking and flashed a warning by lamp that she should heave-to or alter her course. Again and again the pilot repeated the warning, but the *Stadshiedam* paid no heed, evidently not understanding the signals. She was now dangerously close to the mines, and the pilot fired a number of coloured lights into the sea in the path of the ship, hoping that this would make the crew appreciate that they were running into danger. Still she sailed on and her destruction seemed to be certain when, as a last resort, the pilot opened fire with his front machine-gun across her bows. At last the crew grasped the situation ; the ship was swung hard to port and away from the mines, which were subsequently destroyed by a British naval vessel.

Convoys and Flying Boats

For the work of convoying merchant vessels the Sunderland flying boat has shown itself to be particularly suitable, with its range of nearly 3,000 miles and its endurance of twelve hours or more. A day's patrol of 1,700 miles is quite normal. With its eight 250-lb. bombs and its seven machine-guns the Sunderland is quite capable of dealing either with a lurking submarine or an adventurous raider in the air. Mines, too, have to be detected and made innocuous. A wide range of sea around the path of the convoy must be searched and closely scanned. The crew—eleven in all —must be constantly on the watch for hidden dangers below. At times there may be boredom, a feeling that nothing will ever happen, but still the men at their stations must not relax their vigilance. They must be careful, too, not to betray the position of the convoy to the enemy. If a radio signal has to be sent to the land, it must be sent from a point hundreds of miles from the place where the convoyed vessels happen to be.

The Sunderland is a four-engined flying boat. A new two-engined flying boat, the Saro-Lerwick, is now coming into service. It will carry on the tradition established by its fine predecessors, the Southampton and the London, both twin-engined flying boats. The other aircraft in use in the Coastal Command are the Avro Anson and the American-built Lockheed Hudsons. That the Coastal Command has also a number of Wellington bombers and long-range fighters (which would be Blenheims) on its establishment was first disclosed in the announcement by the Air Ministry of the raid conducted on the night of 11th April, 1940, against Stavanger air base. It was a patrol of three Lockheed Hudsons which located the " prison-ship " *Altmark* in the Josing Fjord, and thus enabled the British seamen on board to be rescued, on 17th February, 1940. The aircraft continued their good work by escorting the *Cossack* and other warships on their journey back to Scotland. Four mines were sighted by the aircraft directly in the paths of the warships when they were a few miles from the Scottish coast. Two of the mines were sunk by the aircraft's machine-gun fire, the other two were dealt with by the destroyers. It was an enormous satisfaction to the Coastal Command to feel that it had had a hand in this Elizabethan episode of the twentieth century.

The Coastal Command has had its share of both bombing and fighting in this war. Aircraft of the Command have engaged and shot down a number of enemy aircraft of both marine and land types. For instance, one of them brought down a Heinkel He 115 seaplane off the east coast of Scotland on 1st January, 1940. Another, a Sunderland flying boat, engaged six

SARO-LERWICK
This high-speed long-range flying boat has two Bristol Hercules 14-cylinder sleeve-valve engines and three power-operated gun turrets.

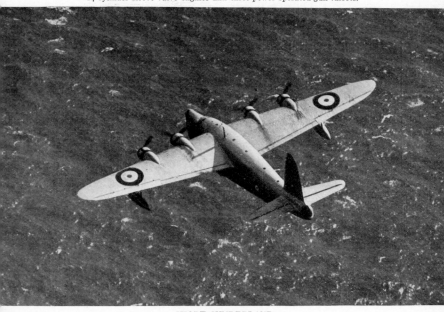

SHORT SUNDERLAND
An unusual view of one of Britain's largest flying boats on patrol.

TORPEDO
BOMBERS

Fifteen Torpedo Bombers, lined up ready to be loaded with torpedoes, during aero-naval exercises on the South Coast.

(Photo : Keystone)

of the formidable Junkers Ju 88 bombers on 3rd April off the Norwegian coast, shot down one of them and so damaged another that it had to come down in Norway (then neutral). Another Sunderland actually shot down a Messerschmitt Me 110 on 27th April in the same waters. An Anson of the Coastal Command repeated the latter very notable feat on 18th July. Perhaps an even more remarkable achievement was that of three Ansons which shot down two of nine German Messerschmitts in a running fight off the Dutch coast on 1st June and disabled two others, sustaining no loss whatever themselves. (Ansons are almost obsolete.) On the same day three Lockheed Hudsons of the Coastal Command engaged forty bombers which were about to attack the transports at Dunkirk and shot down three of them (Junkers Ju 87's) ; two others were damaged and the rest driven off —and the Hudsons escaped without even a bullet hole. Hudsons have done much useful work in attacks on ground targets too. They bombed the oil tanks at Hamburg and Bremen on the night of 18th May. Two nights later Coastal Command were again poaching in the reserves of the Bombing Command. They attacked the oil refinery and fuel tanks at Rotterdam on the night of 20th May in brilliant moonlight, which made it easy to locate the target ; fires caused by the bombs soon made it easier still. Four tanks were set ablaze and so was the refinery. The raiders had to fly through a terrific barrage of shrapnel and flaming onions, but only one of them sustained any damage and that was slight. Four nights later they attacked the tanks at Rotterdam again. The pilot of one of the last aircraft taking part in this raid reported that a row of oil tanks was burning fiercely when he arrived. It must have burned for four days, for when the Coastal Command aircraft made a further raid on the tanks on 26th May they found fires still alight. They added their contribution to the conflagration. " High up on our way," said a pilot, " we could see that the whole area was a red, glowing mass. Wharves, docks and plant all seemed to be burning as well." Another of the objectives of the Hudsons of the Coastal Command was the aerodrome at Vaernes near Trondheim, used by the Germans. They bombed it very thoroughly on the night of 19th May, making many craters in the landing ground and setting hangars and other buildings well ablaze.

THE FLEET AIR ARM

The circumstances of the war brought it about that for the first eight months of the war the Coastal Command had almost stolen the show from the naval air branch, its partner in the aerial policing of the sea. Only occasional glimpses were caught of the latter service. We heard of it in connection with the glorious action of the River Plate. It was a Fairey Sea Fox seaplane catapulted from the *Ajax* which sighted the *Graf Spee* and played an important part in the drama which culminated in the pocket battleship's scuttling. (The pilot of the Sea Fox, Lieut. E. D. G. Lewin, was subsequently awarded the Distinguished Service Cross.) We heard of it again in the operations on the Norwegian coast in April, 1940. It played a wonderful part there, protecting our ships and men, destroying all the hangars at Vaernes and other objectives on land, bombing enemy supply ships and shooting down at least ten enemy aircraft—a wonderful performance for ship-based against shore-based aircraft. Well was the Admiralty's signal of congratulation merited : " We are proud of the Fleet Air Arm." Splendid work was done also by the Fleet Air Arm after the German offensive began in May and thereafter in the Mediterranean and Atlantic as well as in the North Sea. The naval airmen took part in all kinds of operations, from harassing the enemy troops when they reached the Channel to bombing ships in Oran, Tobruk, Dakar and other ports, in addition to carrying on their ordinary duty of observation for the Fleet.

The inner ring of the air defence of our maritime communications is kept by the Coastal Command, the outer by the Fleet Air Arm. The one, like the other, is an auxiliary of the Navy in so far as its task is the defence of sea-borne commerce. The closest co-operation between the two services is essential if the defence is to be effective. In the House of Commons on 7th March, 1940, Sir Kingsley Wood explained the machinery of co-ordination which had been established for this purpose. The naval Commander-in-Chief of the various naval areas and the Air Officers Commanding the Groups of the Coastal Command shared the same headquarters, he stated, and their responsibilities extended over the same areas. The closest co-operation between the two services was ensured by the special appointment of an Air Marshal and of an Admiral whose task it was constantly to review in consultation the operational situation in the North Sea and round our coasts, and to advise their respective Chiefs of Staff. The Admiralty maintained the closest liaison not only with the Coastal Command but also with the Bomber and Fighter Commands. It was only a matter of seconds for direct contact to be established between the First Sea Lord or the Naval Staff and the Commanders-in-Chief of the Air Force Commands.

AIR AND SEA

Because it serves sea power also the Coastal Command is not the less a vital link in the chain of air power. The appointed sphere of its activities lies, physically, between the battle zones of the Bomber and the Fighter Commands. It is a girdle of defence encircling Britain but strands from the two other Commands' defensive fabrics are to be discerned passing through it here and there. It has no monopoly of the air warfare that is carried on above the focal or terminal waters around our coasts. Bombers may take a hand no less than aircraft of the Coastal Command in operations against submarines. Fighters may venture out to sea to engage enemy aircraft attacking merchant or fishing vessels. The three Commands fulfil their parts in ensuring that the traffic lanes are kept open, that shipping can enter and leave our ports, that there is no interruption in the flow of trade which is the life-blood of our existence as an island people.

It is predominantly, however, the Coastal Command which is the air patrol of the narrow seas, the air police which safeguards the maritime approaches to our coasts. In performing its allotted tasks it is the ally or auxiliary of the Navy but it renders at the same time to the Air Force a service which is of direct and funda-

TORPEDO
An aircraft of the Fleet Air Arm discharging a torpedo.
(*Photo : Central Press Photos Ltd., London*)

END OF A
DORNIER
This Dornier flying
boat was shot down
in the North Sea in
35 seconds by a
Hudson reconnais-
sance aircraft of the
Coastal Command.
This photograph was
taken from the
Hudson.

(*Official Photograph*)

mental importance. It helps the Navy to ensure that the Air Force continues to be an Air Force. It would cease to be one if its supplies of petrol were stopped, and most of those supplies come from overseas. The Air Force would be immobilised if they were cut off. In this respect the Coastal Command is a vital element in the organic whole of British air power.

There is no conflict here, it will be seen, between British sea power and British air power. There *is* a conflict between British sea power and enemy air and sea power in combination. To meet this challenge sea power must call air power to its aid, and the call, we may be assured, will not go unheard. Nothing that has happened in this war gives us reason to fear that the challenge will be successful. Neither from above nor from below is sea power likely to be overthrown in its own domain. It may have to fight hard to retain its mastery. The peak of the struggle has not been reached as yet. But the signs and tokens are already clear. British sea power will not be broken by enemy sea or air power. The result will be, from one point of view, a defeat for air power, but from another it will be a triumph, for air power will itself have been enlisted in the fight on behalf of sea power.

CHAPTER 9

AIR FORCE OVERSEAS

SOUTH AND EAST

AT home the organisation of the Air Force has a functional basis. Abroad, it has a geographical basis. There are headquarters of the Royal Air Force, under Air Officers Commanding, in the Middle East, Palestine and Transjordan, Iraq, India, Mediterranean (Malta), Aden, and the Far East (Singapore and Hong Kong).[1] In some of these areas wars and *semi*-wars have come and gone during the last twenty-two years. The Air Force has been in action more than once in the Aden Protectorate, in Palestine, on the Indian North-West frontier. There has been no lack of variety in the life of our squadrons on the fringes of Empire. They have shown themselves to be " handy men " in the air. They have had to suppress rebellions that came to life, to stifle others before birth, to check incipient revolt by showing their wings, to bring encouragement to friendly tribes threatened by lawless neighbours, to

[1] Only passing reference is made here to these Overseas Commands, apart from those in France, the Far East and the Middle East. Further information can be obtained in recent publications by two well-known aeronautical writers : *The Air Force of To-day*, by Mr. E. Colston Shepherd (Blackie) ; *British Aviation*, by Major F. A. de V. Robertson (Longmans Green for the British Council).

search for missing air liners, to succour travellers marooned in the desert, to transport whole battalions of troops from command to command. In the winter of 1928–29 they conveyed 586 people by air from Kabul to India, crossing mountains of 10,000 feet altitude in bitter cold and losing not a machine nor a person in the process. There has been plenty of the kind of work which calls for endurance, cool judgment, initiative, reliability. It has been well and faithfully done. The activities of the Air Force overseas have been the means of keeping its members fit for the sterner trial of a major war.

The most important of the overseas Commands is, normally, the Middle East. Strategically, it is admirably placed. It is in a key position for the purposes alike of offensive action and of prompt reinforcement. Its area extends from the Mediterranean in the north to the Sudan and East Africa in the south, and from the frontier of Italian Libya in the west to the borders of Saudi Arabia in the east. It is mostly fine country for flying. The climate is excellent, from the airman's point of view. It is within easy reach, by air, of other commands of the Royal Air Force. Reinforcements from Iraq, Aden, Malta and India could be assembled in Egypt within a matter of hours. Petrol supply would present no difficulty even if communications with the west were interrupted. Cairo has been called the " Clapham Junction of the air." It might also be regarded as the pivot upon which the long mechanical arm of British air power can turn and swing in wide circles over Europe, Asia and Africa. It has come prominently into the picture since Italy declared war on 10th June. Since then our

Air Force in Egypt has been continuously in action, as has also the South African Air Force operating from Kenya, where the Southern Rhodesian Air Force has been in action as well.

The Far East Command, which embraces Hong Kong, has its headquarters at Singapore and is another overseas Command of great strategic importance. The Air Force there stretches out a hand to India and Iraq in the north-west and to Australia in the south-west. Seletar, on the north shore of the island of Singapore, is one of the great air bases of the Empire and another junction in the radiating lines of British air power. Its importance is increasing. At the end of the present war Australia will be in the position of a major Power in the air ; her strength will be at least as great as that of any of the great Powers of a decade ago. From Darwin the air passage to Singapore can be accomplished without a stop. Both reinforcements for the units of the Royal Air Force there and of the local Volunteer Air Force and the provision of equipment for them, at need, from the greatly developed Australian sources of supply would present no great difficulty. Australia, in turn, stands to benefit from the proximity of the Royal Air Force to the Royal Australian Air Force in this area. The mobility of the air arm here, as elsewhere, gives imperial defence an advantage which supplements that which sea power has long afforded to the British Commonwealth of Nations.

B.E.F.

It was in France, however, that the Royal Air Force overseas had its centre of gravity until the collapse of the French resistance on 17th June. The Air Force there was composed of two elements. There was, first, the "Air Component" of the British Expeditionary Force, that is to say, the co-operation aircraft and fighters assigned for duty with the army. There was, secondly, the "Advanced Air Striking Force," composed of bomber and fighter squadrons. The latter force was furnished by the Bomber Command and was subject for the first four months of the war to the control of the Air Officer Commanding-in-Chief the Bomber Command. In January, 1940, however, a change was made in the organisation. It was necessitated, the official announcement stated, by the increase in the strength of the Army in France and the need for affording the necessary co-operation and support to the Army. A new Command was accordingly formed, "British Air Forces in France," to control both the Air Component and the Advanced Air Striking Force. The new Air Officer Commanding-in-Chief would be responsible, it was stated, in consultation with the Army Commanders-in-Chief, for ensuring the most effective support by the Royal Air Force for the British Expeditionary Force and the French Armies on the western front. The arrangement involved no change, it was added, in the principle governing the relationship between the Army and the Royal Air Force ; it was based on the analogy of the existing relationship between the Royal Navy and the Coastal Command of the Royal Air Force, and would ensure the closest co-operation between the Army and the air forces in the field.

The effect of the change was to withdraw the Advanced Air Striking Force from the control of the

Bomber Command in England, and to that extent the new arrangement was open to criticism as tending to impair the cohesion of the counter-offensive arm of the Royal Air Force. On the other hand, it ensured that all the British air units in France would be under a single direction if the need for combined action should arise, it overcame the difficulty that the Air Component was more or less immobilised whenever the Army was inactive, and it facilitated staff and administrative work in various ways.

AIR AND THE ARMY

The need for powerful air support for the operations of land forces has been one of the lessons taught by recent wars. In theory the Army has its own specialised aircraft, or at least, if not its own, aircraft entirely at its disposal. These, the army co-operation machines, Westland Lysanders at present, are admirable machines of their kind. They have a remarkable rate of climb and are easy to handle. They can shoot up from the ground almost rocketwise and can land in a very much restricted space. With their " parasol " wings, controllable pitch airscrews, and Handley Page flaps and slots they are capable of a very rapid take-off and, when in the air, of maintaining flight at a very low speed ; they remain under full flying control at only fifty-five miles per hour, a great advantage for observation of ground objects. They have a particularly good field of vision as a result of the position of the cabin and the depth of the transparent sides. Their weakness is that they are distinctly slow. With the Bristol Perseus XII engine the Lysander's maximum speed at 15,000 feet is only 230 miles per hour, that is, more than a hundred miles per hour less than that of most present-day fighters and fifty to seventy miles per hour less than the top speed of some bombers. The armament of the Lysander, consisting of two (fixed) machine-guns firing forward and operated by the pilot and a third (movable) gun behind him, operated by the observer, is, again, no match for the powerful battery of a modern fighter. The need for a stiffening of the Air Component by the addition of fighter machines is obvious. There were, in fact, Hurricane squadrons with the Air Component as well as some Blenheim bombers.[1]

Bombers are needed, too, for work with the Army. Ground defences have become so powerful that the sole hope of successful penetration is to smother them with high explosives, and the aircraft is able to supplement the big gun in this task. It can help an army to blast a way through a strongly prepared position. We have seen recently how the Russian bombers assisted the tanks and artillery in the assaults upon the Mannerheim Line and enabled their ground troops to force a way through the Karelian Isthmus. Fighters, too, can take a part in such tactical operations. In Poland, as a military correspondent pointed out in *The Times* of 11th September, 1939, the close co-operation of the German air force with the ground forces had very important results. " In direct attack," he wrote, " the employment of low-flying aircraft has been possible for the Germans. Such tactics, which were still in their infancy in 1918, were found in the later stages of the Spanish war to be highly effective. It will take

[1] There were also two Hurricane Squadrons with the Advanced Air Striking Force, as well as Battle and Blenheim bombers.

little imagination on the part of any man who has had experience of warfare to picture the difficulties of facing the combined attack of armoured fighting vehicles and low-flying aircraft, especially when this attack is also supported by artillery in superior strength."

This correspondent, it will be observed, refers to the employment of low-flying aircraft in Spain. In Spain, the air arm took a direct and influential part in the ground operations. "The main use of aircraft by both sides," says a British writer who served as an officer in the Spanish Foreign Legion (Nationalist), " has been against the enemy's army in the field, to supplement the deficiency in artillery, especially heavy artillery. Nationalist aviation, in particular, has played a decisive part in almost all offensives by carrying out heavy bombing and low-flying machine-gun attacks upon the enemy troops in the front line."[1]   In Spain, says Herr von Poturzyn, " the air arm won important successes in the ground fighting. It maintained the tradition established in Abyssinia and helped to bring about decisions. Apart from its task in provisioning isolated detachments of ground troops (at the Alcazar in Toledo and a number of invested monasteries and barracks), it has taken an immediate part in the infantry engagements. Before each infantry advance the air arm has sprayed the enemy's front lines with machine-gun bullets and light explosive bombs and has been able to paralyse the enemy's resistance during the short time necessary for the infantry attack to be successfully launched."[2]   Von Poturzyn quotes General Armengaud

[1] Peter Kemp, " Some Lessons of the Spanish War," in *National Review*, February, 1939.
[2] F. von Poturzyn, *Luftmacht*, p. 86.

AVRO ANSONS

Reconnaissance aircraft flying in formation above the clouds.

(Photo: *Central Press Ltd., London*)

ON THE
WESTERN FRONT
A fighter squadron
of the R.A.F. on
patrol above the
clouds and ready to
pounce on any Ger-
man aircraft.

(*Official Photograph*)

as saying that " the decisive results of the first attacks are undoubtedly the work of the air arm."[1]

LESSONS FROM SPAIN AND FRANCE

An American military eye-witness has described the technique of air support as it was practised in Spain. Bombers with small bombs and machine-guns would first rake the enemy trenches from a height of about 150 feet, passing along them in single file, or *la cadena*, as it was called, and meanwhile the tanks and the infantry would deploy for the assault, which followed before the defenders had recovered from the initial attack from the air. The bombers used for this purpose were usually Heinkel 48's, carrying two machine-guns and thirty small bombs ; they were slow machines, but this was no disadvantage for the particular purpose of ground attack. They were protected by chaser planes flying high in the sky.[2] " The method at present used in Spain," wrote a British officer, " is that successive waves of aircraft dive on the defensive positions, dropping a shower of light bombs and raking the area with machine-gun fire. Before the effect of this action has had time to wear off, the positions are assaulted by the infantry."[3] When the positions assaulted had been carried the air arm still had work to do. In pursuit, as Marshal Badoglio has testified, it has proved itself to be " a particularly devastating arm."[4]

[1] F. von Poturzyn, *Luftmacht*, p. 86.
[2] Brig. Gen. H. J. Reilly, " The Aeroplane's Role in Battle in Spain," in *The Aeroplane*, 26th April, 1939.
[3] Brig. Gen. A. B. Beauman, *A Short Outline of Modern Tactics*, 1939, p. 45.
[4] Pietro Badoglio, Marshal of Italy, Duke of Addis Ababa, *The War in Abyssinia*, 1937, pp. 85, 119.

More than three years before the present war began, Wing Commander (now Air Commodore) J. C. Slessor drew attention to the importance of close co-operation between aircraft and ground forces. He challenged the fashionable assumption that the war of the future would be " inevitably an affair of lethal gases and bacilli rained from the air exclusively upon the female and non-combatant sections of the population in open towns."[1] It was more probable, he held, that the first call upon the air arm would be to support the army in the decisive theatre of war. Its objectives would be the enemy forces, their lines of communication and their system of supply, and it would have its definite contribution to make to any decision on land.[2] His words have been amply confirmed by the events of the present war. When the storm broke on the western front in May, 1940, the spearhead of the German advance was the air arm. In close co-operation with tanks and mechanised forces it smashed a way through the defences on the Dutch and Belgian frontiers and opened the gap on the Meuse which enabled a deep penetration to be effected into French territory. A British war correspondent has given us the Belgian General Daumerie's account of the way in which the attack began in the Lanaeken-Eben-Eymael sector.

At four o'clock on 10th May, he said, many German aeroplanes were reported flying over the Belgian positions, which were fully manned. " Ten minutes later, without the slightest warning, hell broke loose. Nothing he experienced throughout the last war could be compared in intensity with this infernal aerial

[1] J. C. Slessor, *Air Power and Armies*, 1936, Introduction, p. viii.
[2] *Ibid.*, pp. 70, 214.

bombardment. The Germans knew exactly where the battalion commands were situated and wiped them out. By the time the bombardment ceased there was little left of the Belgian defences." A worse surprise was to come when hundreds of parachutists began to drop from aircraft behind the Belgian lines, while the remaining defenders were too dazed to shoot them down as they descended. It was disguised parachutists who apparently prevented the bridges over the Albert Canal at Kessel and Vroenhoven from being demolished; others put the big guns in the fortress of Eben-Eymael out of action.[1]

In the break-through north of Sedan the German aircraft also played the leading part. " It is the tanks which caused the break-through on the Meuse," wrote the military correspondent of *The Times* on 18th May; " but the tanks without the accompanying aircraft and, above all, without the dive-bombers, would not have been particularly formidable. In some cases the tanks did not persist in face of strong resistance, but they quickly returned to the assault directly they obtained fresh support in the air. The bombs probably do not cause heavy losses to troops in the open, but they have a temporarily stunning effect, even when no one is hit, and such moments afford the tank its opportunity. The Germans have also used delayed-action bombs, so that a position is, as it were, kept under bombardment for some time after the aircraft have passed. In certain parts of the front the French infantry were at least temporarily shaken by the weight of these combined air and armoured assaults, with the result that whole

[1] Mr. H. Carleton Greene in the *Daily Telegraph*, 18th May, 1940.

columns of smaller detachments of tanks broke clean through."

If enemy aircraft were foremost in the attack, our own aircraft, alike of the Advanced Air Striking Force and of the Air Component, were vigorously active in the defence. Apart from raids upon roads, bridges and railways behind the enemy's lines, they attacked his tanks, mechanised columns and troops on the march with bombs and machine-gun fire. They hampered and harassed him at many points. They destroyed pontoon bridges, blocked roads, interrupted the service of supply and reinforcement. They suffered heavily themselves in their daring attacks, pressed home against fierce opposition. A squadron of Blenheims lost eleven machines, for example, when it attacked a key position at Gembloux on 17th May. Next day we had full revenge, when nine Hurricanes attacked twenty Junkers Ju 87's and shot down ten of them. In all these engagements we bagged three enemy aircraft for each British machine lost, and on the average forty enemy aircraft a day were brought down by our fighters during May. On two days, 27th and 29th May, the bags were fifty and seventy-seven certainties and many "probables," and on later days the bag was hardly less.

VICTORY AT DUNKIRK

It was on the tormented beaches of Dunkirk at the end of May that the first great trial of strength occurred between the British and the German Air Forces. "There was a victory inside the deliverance," said Mr. Churchill in the House of Commons on 4th June, in

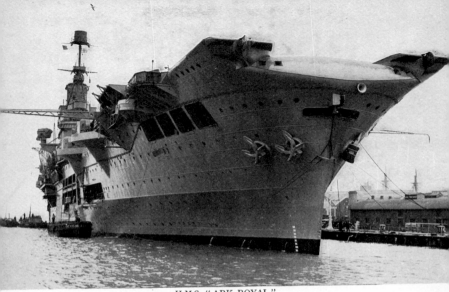

H.M.S. "ARK ROYAL"
The great aircraft-carrier refuelling at a home port.

WITH THE FLEET AIR ARM
A Skua is shown taking off from the flight deck of an aircraft-carrier.
The central tower is on the right.
(Photo : Topical Press Agency Ltd.

FOOD FROM THE AIR

How the Royal Air Force would solve the problem of getting food supplies to marooned and beleaguered parties. The pilot of a Westland Lysander army co-operation aircraft loading up a food canister, which can be dropped by parachute.

A FLEEING DORNIER

The Blenheim, from which this photograph was taken, encountered a Dornier flying boat over the North Sea. The Dornier is seen skimming the waves in a desperate attempt to escape. A few seconds later it was destroyed.

(Official Photograph

his speech upon the evacuation of our army from Dunkirk. " It was gained by the Air Force," " Our Air Force decisively defeated the main strength of the enemy Air Force and inflicted upon the enemy losses of at least four to one." In that success, as Mr. Churchill said, we can find " a sure basis upon which practical and reassuring thoughts may rest."

His optimistic forecast has been reinforced by the success of our defence in repelling attacks upon our coasts and shipping since he spoke. During July at least 240 German aircraft were brought down by our fighters and anti-aircraft guns, the most on any single day being 28. July's total had been passed by mid-August, and our fighters' bag for all August was 964 German aircraft.

Britain is building up a great Army as well as a great Air Force. She will be again by 1942, as she was in 1917–18, a first-class military Power. The magnitude of her effort on land can be judged from the fact that she had nine ordnance factories before the present war started and will have fifty-three in 1941. The Army which needs all these establishments to supply it with guns, shells, rifles and ammunition will be an immense one. It will be one which will need an exceedingly large number of air squadrons for co-operation with it. Army co-operation means to-day, for an air force, more than it meant in the last war. It means throwing air power as unstintingly as land power into the crucible whose fiery product is victory. There is not a shadow of doubt that we shall have the men and the machines needed for that final trial of strength in the air.

CHAPTER 10

PAST AND FUTURE

THE BOWMEN BEGAN IT

THE subject of this book is British air power. That is, by itself, a rather vague and almost meaningless expression. It becomes clearer and less intangible when one splits up air power into power to bomb, to fight, to reconnoitre, to co-operate with fleets and armies. It means, in fact, the exercise of the functions falling to the Bomber Command, the Fighter Command, the Coastal Command, and the British Air Forces in theatres of war oversea.

British sea power is a known quantity. We have thought for generations of England as a nation of seamen. It was by using the sea that she became great. Her strength was drawn from the sea. We are inclined to forget that it was not always so. The origins of her greatness are not to be traced along the highways of the ocean. It was not as seamen but as *aerial bombadiers* —of a primitive kind—that English soldiers first made themselves feared on the battlefields of Europe. That seems to be a paradox, an historical impossibility, yet it is true.

There was no English fleet in the fourteenth and fifteenth centuries. There was none, indeed, until the days of Henry VII. Britain's sea power was a creation of a later century. Her earliest renown was won on land. At Crecy, Edward III had an army which was regarded as utterly unorthodox in those days of chivalry. It contained eleven to twelve thousand archers and less than four thousand men-at-arms, with some light forces : an intolerable deal of archers, the conservative soldiers of that age would have said. Philip of France had on his side an army nearly twice as large but of the feudal pattern. It had only a small proportion of archers—Genoese cross-bowmen ; and the cross-bow was no match for the long-bow in the hands of a yeoman from the English shires. At Poictiers, again, the archers were the bulk of the Black Prince's army, which was less than half the French king's in numbers, and again the French, though they had more bowmen on this occasion, relied mainly on their armoured knights. At Agincourt the Constable of France, D'Albret, had but few bowmen ; he had declined the offer of the citizens of Paris to send him many. Henry V had six thousand archers and only a thousand men-at-arms (including " my cousin Westmoreland," Bedford and Exeter, Warwick and Talbot, and all the rest), and he was outnumbered by four to one. It was because men-at-arms were a mere historical survival and the bowman was the winner of battles that the English triumphed. What decided the day was *bombardment*—artillery, if you like, but it is permissible to choose the analogy which suits one's subject and to say *aerial*. There is no difference in principle between the missile launched from the gun and from the aircraft.

When one thinks of those old battles one should

picture to oneself the rain of deadly arrows, the air full of them, the dense ranks powerless to escape them or to come to grips with the foe. One can imagine the twang and whistle of them as they were sped from the English bows. "And over me and round me were the grey geese flying." It was the grey goose wing that won in 1346, 1356 and 1415. To-day, again, the grey geese of England are on the wing. They are faring forth from Lincoln, Norfolk, Suffolk—geese that fly far and wide, that show their wings over far-distant fields, that fly at speeds thrice as great as the swiftest bird's. The airmen of Britain are making history to-day as the bowmen of Britain did then.

Human flight is less than a generation old. The Wrights' first successful attempts were made only in 1904. The Channel was flown only in 1909. It is hardly surprising that in the war of 1914–18 the aerial arm had not found itself. It is amazing that it should have accomplished even as much as it did accomplish. By the end of the war there were great and, for that time, powerful air forces in being. The greatest and most powerful was the British Air Force. In quality and in numbers it had established its claim to hold " the right of the line." It will be entitled to hoist the whip at the fore before this war ends, too.

In the years that followed the Royal Air Force dwindled in numbers. It became a shadow of what it had been. At least, however, the organisation which had been established in 1917–18 was maintained, and the high standard which had been set was not relaxed. When, reluctantly, belatedly, we began to rearm in 1935–36 we had sound foundations upon which to build. We had no need to improvise, to experiment, to create *ab initio*. We had merely to expand. Reflation of the British Air Force succeeded deflation ; that was all.

Fortunately, we had in this country a well-established engineering industry which was able and willing to turn to the production of the all-metal aircraft which had now succeeded the wooden machines of the last war. (Furniture-making firms had largely filled the gap in 1916–18.) We had also an experienced reserve of skilled labour which soon adapted itself to the new technique of construction. Machine-tools were more readily obtainable than in the former war. Aluminium and the hardening metals were abundantly available. In three years, 1936 to 1939, very considerable improvement was recorded in the output of both airframes and aero engines, though even by the latter date we were still far from having the lead in production.[1] When the war began we were, comparatively, more or less at the same stage, as regards organisation of aeronautical supply, as we were in the summer of 1917, that is, at the time of the formation of the second (Lord Cowdray's) Air Board. We were in a position to " go full steam ahead " ; which we did, promptly. We were in a better position than at that time, indeed, because we had taken steps to promote production in the Dominions. The amendment of the American Neutrality Act of 1st May, 1937, a couple of months after the war began was another important advantage. Mr. Churchill was able to state on 20th August, 1940,

[1] Some rather absurd statements were made about our output before the war, e.g., that over 1,000 machines a month were being produced in the summer of 1939.

that though the enemy still had a more numerous air force, " our new production already largely exceeds his, and the American production is only just beginning to flow in."

The danger was that the supply of trained *personnel* might not keep pace with that of *matériel*. An even larger reserve of airmen than of machines is needed to make good the wastage of war. The monthly wastage rate of machines may be anything from 50 to 100 per cent. in active operations.[1] It would be much less, of course, if air warfare were only of a guerrilla nature. Now that the air war has become intensive the replacement of the crews of bombers is a problem which all the belligerents may have difficulty in solving. The crew of a bomber consists of from two to six men, and each crash in enemy territory, or otherwise involving a total loss, means, therefore, a far greater demand upon the reserve of airmen than upon the reserve of machines. Air crews cannot be trained overnight, and the formation of a deep reserve of *personnel* is imperative if raiding operations are not to be brought to a standstill.

The formation of the Royal Air Force Volunteer Reserve in 1936 went some way towards creating the necessary pool of pilots and observers, but with the coming of war some still bolder approach to the problem was found to be necessary. The flying training schools were becoming congested. There were bottle-necks

[1] A wastage rate of " at least 50 per cent. " is mentioned in the pamphlet " Assurance of Victory," p. 15, issued by the Ministry of Information in December, 1939. In the *Air Annual of the British Empire*, 1938, Major Oliver Stewart stated that Lord Trenchard had calculated the wastage rate in war at 80 per cent. in 1925, but now expert opinion is inclined to put the wastage at 100 per cent. per month.

RHEINE,
WESTPHALIA

(a) New Barracks.
(b) Railway line to
Munster. (c) Railway
line to Emden. (d)
Railway line to Osna-
bruck. (e) Station.
(f) Other railways.
(g) River Ems. (h)
Sports ground. (i)
Shadow of church
spire. (j) Long
shadow of a very
tall spire.

(Official Photo by
R.A.F)

A GERMAN
AERODROME,
LANGEN HAEGEN
AERODROME,
HANOVER.
Photographed by
R.A.F.

(a) Quarters. (b)
Special railway line.
(c) Station and plat-
form. (d) Hangars.
(e) Motor transport.
(f) Oil patches made
by aircraft parked
always at the same
spot. (g) Servicing
tarmac. (h) Runway.
(i) Aircraft moving
off across aerodrome.

(Photo: News Agen-
cies Ltd., London))

here and there in the instructional channel. A wider source of supply of air crews was sought, and it was found in the Empire air training scheme which was inaugurated in the autumn of 1939. The help of the Dominions was enlisted and an immense programme of air training in Canada, Australia, New Zealand and other British possessions was actively organised. "When in full operation," said Sir Kingsley Wood on 7th March, 1940, "the schools in Canada, Australia and New Zealand under the Empire training scheme will produce no less than 20,000 pilots and 30,000 air crews every year. In addition, the Government of the Union of South Africa have most helpfully offered to train pilots, and there also will be schools in Rhodesia and in Kenya." He and the Prime Ministers of Canada and Australia had spoken, when the scheme was first announced in October, 1939, of the determination of the participants to create "air forces of overwhelming strength."

They will all be needed. The tasks to be performed are many. Broadly, they fall into three main categories : to hold and shatter an air attack upon the heart of the Empire ; to keep the seaways which are the veins and arteries of the Empire's body open ; to bring the might of the Empire's air arm to bear upon the issue of a continental struggle. The first task has proved hitherto a light one but it may not always be so. We may still have to meet and break the menace to this island, and we shall break it : of that there is no shadow of doubt. So, too, we will smash every attempt to cut our maritime communications. The Navy and the Coastal Command will see to that—as they have seen to it already. It is in the third task that the heaviest demand of all may be made upon the resources of Britain's air power. The supreme struggle for mastery in the air is yet to come. The Empire's great air fleet will go singing into that fight, as Don John of Austria and his young captains went singing into Lepanto, for this, too, will be a brave adventure that is at the same time a crusade.

An immense number of squadrons—bombers, fighters, reconnaissance—will be needed for all these varied services. The tasks which the vast British air power now taking shape will be called upon to perform will be manifold. The bowmen of Creçy or Agincourt had a single task : to stand firm in the line and shoot straight. The airman's task is far more varied. A differently trained man and a specialised machine are needed for each kind of service : for the long-range offensive that is still defence because it slakes down the volume of hostile attack that can be launched against ourselves ; for the short-range work, which is defence in the narrow sense, against air invasion ; for the policing of the tide-water channels encompassing our shores ; for the localised air operations required to support the army in a continental theatre of war. The last of these is perhaps the nearest analogy to the old bowman's task, yet how different ! The long-bow was the archer's weapon of all works, and the technique of its use was simple. The modern mechanised archery is composite, complex, functionally differentiated, scientifically adapted to the end in view.

For the long-range raids that start from Britain, for instance, there are the big bombers whose tanks may carry two tons or more of petrol, which can keep the air for ten hours on end, which can load a deadly cargo of bombs in their racks : the Wellingtons, Whitleys, Hampdens, Herefords. They are magnificent riders of the air, these long, clean, streamlined mechanical birds that come roaring out of the north, more strident than whooper swans. There are the Blenheims, too, and the Beauforts, swift and powerful in attack. British air power can hit, hit hard and hit a long distance away while it has these battleships of the clouds at call ; and they do not exhaust our designers' and constructors' genius for capping a rival's best. The jigs and tools for their successors have been prepared long since.

Then there are the machines whose specialty is defence pure and simple, the interceptors, the fighters. Here the range is less, the hitting power in horizontal combat greater. Fighters with longer range than our present Spitfires, Hurricanes and Defiants will be appearing before long, but still the rôle of the aircraft of this category will be primarily interception. The newer fighters will be more deadly killers than the old. We shall have them in thousands.

Bombers and fighters have work to do also in keeping our coastal waters clear of enemy raiders, but it is the sea-going aircraft that is pre-eminently the guardian of the narrow seas. The big flying boats, the coastal reconnaissance landplanes must patrol unceasingly the channels and shipping lanes. Here the Royal Navy and the Coastal Command work in close harmony. Their task is a dual one : to protect our own shipping and to interrupt all such maritime traffic as brings aid and comfort to the foe. If the air warfare against our sea-borne commerce is intensified so we shall bring into action the immense number of machines of *super*-Sunderland, *super*-Anson and *super*-Lockheed type which are already in production.

Bombers, fighters and reconnaissance aircraft are also required in great numbers for tactical work in and around the zones of the land operations. Land power no less than sea power must call air power in aid if it is to cope on equal terms with a foe powerfully equipped with the mechanised instruments of war which science has devised for use by land, sea and air. Britain is creating an army comparable to the strongest in Europe. At the same time an air component of immense proportions is being swiftly created to co-operate with it. It may be indeed that if the issue of the war is decided on land, the decision will depend to a great extent upon the amplitude of the air strength available to the one commander-in-chief or the other. We shall not be in a position of inferiority in that final trial of strength.

British air power means all that is stated or implied here, but it means something more. The work described represents the minimum, the respectable sufficiency of endeavour. Britain does not intend to stop there. The Empire has committed itself to a step more far-reaching still. It is creating an *aerial mass of manœuvre*, a mass extra to all normal requirements, a mass that can be thrown in anywhere, a mass that will be overwhelming, irresistible, an avalanche that renews itself.

We are in face of something new, unknown, without precedent. Air power is beginning to find itself. Our conception of its nature, still half uncomprehended, is coloured inevitably by our old, well-grasped

HUDSONS OVER HELIGOLAND
Two of a formation of these American-built Lockheed-Hudson
aircraft ,which have been equipped with a deadly new gun turret.
(*Official Photograph*)

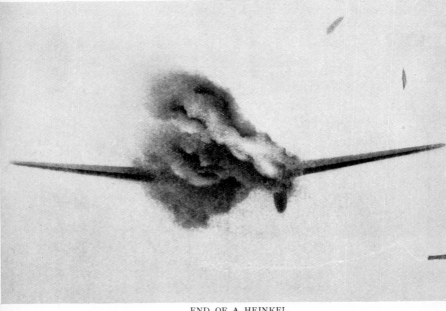

END OF A HEINKEL
A Heinkel iii at the end of a combat just before it crashed in flames. The
engines, fuselage and petrol tanks are all ablaze. The film from which this
picture was taken shows the enemy aircraft disintegrating in mid-air.
(*Photo : P.N.A.*)

THE END OF A GERMAN BOMBER

One of the seven brought down recently in one day near a town in East Anglia. The bullet holes show the good shooting by the ground defences.

Photo: Central Press Photos Ltd.

conception of sea-power. It must be so, for Britain. Britain did not build sea power by half-measures, nor will she so build air power. She tackles big tasks in a big way. The picture which British air power presents to us is, instinctively, one of a vast flotilla of air squadrons sufficient, when all the needs of defence and co-operation on land and sea have been met, to undertake the larger strategical ventures that may well shape the immediate destinies of western Europe. One sees masses of bombers, screened by masses of fighters, moving swiftly, irresistibly forward, along pathways which do not stop short at land frontiers. One sees Britain as mighty in the air as on the sea.

This is what British air power means, the air power that is being fashioned, grimly, remorselessly, by this war-hating, war-winning, Empire of ours.

INDEX

Aandalsnes, the Gladiators at, 117–120
Advanced Air Striking Force, 100, 137, 139, 144
Air Component, 137, 138, 144
Altmark incident, 128
America, *see* United States
Amiot bomber, 61
Armament branch of R.A.F. formed, 86
Armstrong-Whitworth Whitley bomber, 94, 95, 100, 101, 102, 153
Australia and the Empire effort, 43–51
Austrian rout in 1918, 19
Automatic pilot ("George"), 98
Auxiliary Air Force, 78–79
Avro Anson aircraft, 124, 128, 129

Badoglio, P., 141
Baldwin, Earl, 106
Balfour, H. H., 51, 72
Ball, A., 17
Balloon Command, 90
Banks, Sir D., 43
Barker, W. G., 17
Barnwell, F. S., 59
Barratt, Sir A. S., 18
Beaufort bomber, 43, 44, 63, 153
Beauman, A. B., 141
Beaverbrook, Lord, 15, 33, 67
Bell Airacobra fighter, 65
Bishop, W. A., 17
Bloch fighter, 66
Boeing "Flying Fortress," 61
Bolingbroke bomber, 40
Bomber Command, work of, 89–104

Bombers *v.* Fighters, 70–73, 106–7
Boulton & Paul Defiant fighter, 69, 122, 153
Bowhill, Sir F. W., 18
Bremen, raids on, 101, 102, 129
Bristol Blenheim bomber, 30, 59, 63, 64, 94, 139, 144, 153
Bulgarian rout in 1918, 19
Burnett, Sir C. S., 18

Cameron, Sir D., 50
Camm, S., 59, 67
Canada and the Empire air effort, 39–43, 46, 48, 49, 52
Cannon for fighters, 70, 72
Caproni bomber, 61
Carey, G. W. F., 45
Chamberlain, Neville, 35, 54
Chatfield, Lord, 38, 74, 107
Churchill, Winston S., 33, 68, 116, 117, 123, 144, 145, 149
Cinema-camera in aircraft, 114
Coastal Command, work of, 124–133
Collishaw, R., 17
Craven, Sir C., 32
Curtiss fighters, 53, 65, 66, 67

Dallas, R. S., 17
Daumerie, Gen., 142
Directorate-General of Production, 32
Dive-bombing, 91–93, 143
Dominions' air effort, 39–54
Dornier bombers, 63–64
Douglas bombers, 53, 61, 63
Dowding, Sir H. C. T., 18, 110

Dunkirk, air actions at, 121–122, 144–145
Duval, Gen., 107

Eden, Anthony, 47
Eliot, G. F., 15
Ellington, Sir E. L., 39
Empire air effort, 39–54, 150, 151
Engineering branch of R.A.F. formed, 86

Fairbairn, J. V., 50
Fairey Battle bomber, 30, 59, 139; in raid on bridge at Maastricht, 103–104; Sea Fox, 130
Far East Command, 136
Farquhar, A. D., 78, 111
Fedden, A. H. R., 58
Fellowes, P. F. M., 71
Fiat bomber, 61; fighter, 66
Fighter Command, work of, 105–123
Fighter v. Bomber, 70–73, 106–107
Finland, war in, 91, 139
"Flaming onions," 96
Fleet Air Arm, 124, 130, 131
Focke–Wulf fighter, 69
France, air strength in 1918, 13, 20; R.A.F. in, 136–145
Frazer-Nash gun-turret, 60

Gardiner, Sir C. B., 35
Garland, D. E., 104
Germany, air strength in 1918, 13, 20
Gladiators at Aandalsnes, 117–120
Graf Spee, finding of, 130
Gray, T., 104
Great Britain, air strength in 1918, 11, 13, 20, 148; in 1924 and 1934, 25; in 1939, 27
Greene, H. C., 143
Ground staff, training of, 84–86
Group system of production, 34
Gunner, air, training of, 81–82

Hamburg, raids on, 101, 102, 129
Handley Page, F., 40
Handley Page Hampden bomber, 41, 43, 94, 100, 101, 153; Hereford, 153
Hawker Hurricane fighter, 24, 40, 41, 55, 59, 66, 68, 110, 111, 113, 116, 120, 121, 139, 144, 153
Hawker, Lanoe, 17
Heinkel bomber, 62, 71, 111, 122; fighter, 68, 69
Heligoland Bight, raid on, 108
Hoare, Sir S., 25, 32
Houston, Lady, 24

Independent Air Force, 1918, 19, 20, 21
India and air expansion, 51
Initial Training Wings, 81, 82
Inskip, Sir T., 43

Jones, H. A., 36
Junkers bombers, 64, 65, 91, 122, 129, 144

Kemp, P., 140
Kensington Court, rescue of crew, 126
Kiel dockyard, bombing of, 102

Langdon-Davies, J., 112
Leaflets, dropping of, 94
LeO 45 bomber, 61
Lever, Sir S. H., 39, 43, 44
Lewin, E. D. G., 130
Liddell Hart, B. H., 109
Link Trainer, 81, 83
Little, R. A., 17
Lockheed Hudson aircraft, 53, 128, 129
Longmore, Sir A. M., 18, 43
Ludlow-Hewitt, Sir E. R., 18
Lyons, J., 43

Macchi fighter, 66
McCudden, J. T. B., 17
Machine tools, importance of, 28, 35

Mackenzie King, L., 49
Mannock, E., 17
Martin bombers, 53, 63
Mechanics, R.A.F., training of, 84–86
Menzies, R. G., 47, 48, 49
Messerschmitt fighters, 67, 68, 120, 121, 122, 129
Middle East Command, 135
Minelaying by aircraft, 97, 98
Mitchell, R. J., 59
Mitchell, Sir W. G. S., 18
Morane fighter, 66, 67
Morgenthau, H., 15
Motor firms and the shadow factories, 28–31
Mottistone, Lord, 17

Navigators, air, training of, 82
Newall, Sir C. L. N., 18, 71
New Zealand and the Empire air effort, 44, 45, 46, 50–51
Norway, campaign in, 92, 99, 117, 120, 130–131
Nuffield, Lord, 31

Observers, air, training of, 81

Pilots, training of, 79, 80, 81
Pirow, O., 46
Poland, campaign in, 20, 91, 92, 139
Potez reconnaissance bomber, 63
Poulain, D., 107
Precision bombing, 92–93

Reilly, H. J., 141
Richthofen, Baron M., 17
Riverdale, Lord, 32, 51
Robertson, F. A. de V., 134
Rolls-Royce engines, 16, 24, 31, 58, 94
Roosevelt, President F. D., 15
Rougeron, C., 41, 42, 106, 107, 112, 113

Salmon, Sir J. M., 46
Saro-Lerwick flying boat, 128

Savoia-Marchetti bombers, 61
Schemes " F," " L," and " M," 26
Schneider Trophy competition, 24
Sea power and air power, 132–133
Security patrols, 96–98
Seely, Gen., see Mottistone
Shadow factories, 28–31
" Silent approach," 112
Shepherd, E. C., 19, 134
Signals branch, R.A.F., formed, 86
Sinclair, Sir A., 47
Slessor, J. C., 142
South Africa and air expansion, 46, 51
Southern Rhodesia and the Empire air effort, 51
Spanish civil war, 42, 70, 91, 106–107, 140, 141
Split assembly, 34
Stadshiedam, saving of, from mines, 126–127
Stewart, O., 150
Sunderland flying boat, 124, 125, 127, 128, 129
Supermarine Spitfire fighter, 24, 31, 55, 59, 66, 68, 110, 111, 113, 121, 122, 153
Swinton, Lord, 42
Sykes, Sir F. H., 19

Training of the R.A.F., 74–88
Trenchard, Lord, 18, 150
Turkish rout in 1918, 19
Turner, C. C., 67

U-boats sunk by aircraft, 125
United States as source of aeronautical supply, 14, 15, 21, 52–53, 149

Vickers Wellesley aircraft, 60 ; Wellington bomber, 60, 61, 62, 94, 95, 101, 153
Volunteer Reserve, R.A.F., 76, 77, 80, 150

Von Poturzyn, F. A. F., 107, 140, 141

Wallis, B. N., 59
Weir, Lord, 16
Westland Lysander aircraft, 40, 41, 138, 139

Williams, D., 120
Wireless operators, training of, 81
Wirraway aircraft, 44
Wood, Sir K., 26, 27, 32, 33, 34, 35, 41, 42, 48, 55, 56, 67, 77, 87, 107, 111, 131, 151